THE TRAITORS

THE TRAITORS

The Interactive Game Book

Alan Connor

CENTURY

3 5 7 9 10 8 6 4 2

Century
20 Vauxhall Bridge Road
London SW1V 2SA

Century is part of the Penguin Random House group of companies
whose addresses can be found at global.penguinrandomhouse.com.

Penguin
Random House
UK

Text copyright © The Random House Group Ltd, 2023
Foreword copyright © Amanda Lovett, 2023
The Traitors © idtv Film & Video Productions BV and RTL Netherlands, 2023
Licensed by All3Media International Limited
Produced in the UK by Studio Lambert

Alan Connor has asserted his right to be identified as the author of this
Work in accordance with the Copyright, Designs and Patents Act 1988.

First published by Century in 2023

www.penguin.co.uk

A CIP catalogue record for this book is available from the British Library.

ISBN 9781529917635

Typeset in 11.4/14.75pt Dante MT Std
by Jouve (UK), Milton Keynes

Printed and bound in Great Britain by Clays Ltd, Elcograf S.p.A.

The authorised representative in the EEA is Penguin Random House Ireland,
Morrison Chambers, 32 Nassau Street, Dublin D02 YH68

www.greenpenguin.co.uk

TABLE OF CONTENTS

DAYS

MISSIONS

BONUS GAMES

FOREWORD

What does it feel like to be a Traitor?

I can remember the moment I felt the hand on my shoulder that meant I would be spending my time in the Castle as a Traitor. There was shock and nervousness, but also, I have to admit, a fair bit of excitement.

The reason the show caught the imagination of the public, and has become such essential viewing, is that it is a show about something we're all utterly fascinated by: other people.

The premise is simple: twenty-two strangers meet at a remote castle in the Scottish Highlands to work together on a series of daily tasks, both physical and mental, to earn up to £120,000, which will go to the winner (or winners).

The catch is that from the protagonists three are chosen to be Traitors, who meet each evening to select one of the remaining Faithfuls to murder. The Faithfuls can fight back at a Round Table meeting each evening, where they debate everyone's behaviour and then vote to banish someone they suspect to be a Traitor.

But that doesn't capture the psychological drama that unfolds. With every murder and every Round Table vote our game changed shape, as there were fewer and fewer of us, and the dynamics of the relationships changed.

We spend our time making assumptions about others. We all think we can read people, and know when someone is lying, but can we?

I had to be above suspicion, forging bonds and building a family around me, as I told lies to new friends. There was pressure and guilt over the backstabbing, betrayal and double-crossing you have to employ to survive, but there was elation at eliminating a rival who had come too close to unveiling your secret. All the time, my fellow contestants who were Faithful had to try and guess everyone's motives to sniff out guilt, double and even triple bluffs.

And now, you too will have the opportunity to test your abilities in this book. Do you have what it takes to enter the Castle?

Will you follow the path of a Faithful or shroud yourself in the cloak of a Traitor? Will you get them before they get you?

Let the games begin!

Love always,

Amanda Lovett

Welcome, Faithful.

The game is afoot. Are you brave enough to turn the page and enter the world of *The Traitors*?

Do you have what it takes to make the right choices and reach the end of this deadly game?

Will you be Faithful or a Traitor?

This book will present you with a series of decisions as you move through the 12 days it takes to make it to the finale. Beware, the wrong decision could see you banished or murdered.

You can take this journey on your own, or with others, pooling your wisdom to make the right choices. Every day you will be called upon to perform a Mission. You can choose to either play along with others, or skip to the end and continue your journey in the Castle.

The book also has regular breakout Bonus Games, separate to the Missions, which can be played with varying numbers of players, all with a *Traitors* twist. So there will be something for everyone in this book, whether you are reading alone, or looking for games to play with others.

Each day will end with a Round Table, as you try to work out who to banish. And every morning will begin with breakfast, as you wait to see whose absence means they have been murdered.

On the next pages are the fellow Contestants who will join you for this journey. Familiarise yourself with them.

When you are ready, turn to section **1** to start the game.

DRAMATIS PERSONAE

- **Alexis**, 39, Edinburgh (travel website editor)

- **Amrit**, 29, Armagh (on-street fundraiser)

- **Anna**, 72, Whitley Bay (actuary)

- **David**, 49, Henley-upon-Thames (publican)

- **Deb**, 24, Port Talbot (court clerk)

- **Elif**, 22, North London (unemployed)

- **Gabriel**, 43, Anglesey (personal therapist)

- **Gregg**, 29, Salford (writer)

- **Irwin**, 41, Carlisle (pilot)

- **Isla**, 26, Isle of Man (aromatherapy shop owner)

- **Jorge**, 60, Folkestone (dentist)

- **Laure**, 31, Zurich (personal trainer)

- **Luke**, 24, Swanage (quantity surveyor)

- **Nina**, 73, Cork ('retired' florist)

- **Precious**, 28, Skye (student)

- **Rakayah**, 19, Dudley ('in IT')

- **River**, 32, South London (museum guide)

- **Ruby**, 29, York (genome researcher)

- **Steve-O**, 42, Lowestoft (coastguard)
- **Teddy**, 24, South London (crypto podcaster)
- **Tim,** 53, Cornwall (park-keeper)
- **You**

1

DAY 1

The sun beats down as you stand on the manicured lawn. Behind you rise the imposing towers of the Castle. You and 21 strangers. Summoned to play a deadly game of truth and lies. Already, those who happened to be sitting next to each other on the train that brought you here have settled into groups. You overhear fragments of the sorts of muttered conversations strangers have as they get to know each other. Nina (Cork, 73) is clearly into flowers, as she points at a particularly verdant bush and says something in Latin.

You find yourself standing between Luke (Swanage, 24) and Deb (Port Talbot, 24) and are somehow drawn into a conversation about whether white or brown bread is best for toast. Not wanting to be controversial, you say you like both but always save the white slice for last as a 'treat', then regret it when no one laughs and you catch Elif (North London, 22) looking at you a little too intently. But there's no time to dwell on it, as everyone suddenly becomes silent and faces in the same direction.

Your Host addresses you from the steps of the Castle: 'Welcome to you all. I trust you enjoyed your trip. The game is afoot, in fact it has been since you arrived at the railway station. You must learn that every decision here matters. Look behind you.' You all turn as one and see a large rectangle on the ground with a colour spectrum moving from green at one end, to red at the other.

'This colour spectrum is to measure your confidence. Green represents a belief you will be good at this game, and red that you will be terrible, with every range of confidence in between. Go now and stand on the colour that represents your level of confidence. How good do *you* think you'll be?'

What do you do?

- Stand on green. Even though you're actually feeling quite nervous, everyone loves confidence. Turn to **185**.

- Stand somewhere in the middle, best not to stand out, isn't it? Turn to **261**.

- Stand on red. Even though you think you might actually be quite good at this, self-deprecation is charming. Turn to **236**.

2

After the Mission, you wander along the corridor, thinking about how only a few days earlier it was almost impossible to find somewhere that people weren't. But now it feels empty. You aren't entirely sure which you prefer, just that at every stage there have been different challenges. You listen to the sound of the Castle creaking in the heat of the sun. Out of the window you watch clouds moving over distant hills.

During the Mission, you tried to watch everyone closely, especially River and Tim, but they didn't seem to be behaving differently in any way. Gabriel was his usual beaming self. Gregg was still a little withdrawn, but understandably so. It feels odd to have your secret and you realise this might be a tiny taster of what it's like to be a Traitor.

You hear the sound of laughter in the corridor and when you stick your head around the door, Gabriel says, 'Hooray, come and play a game with us!'

- Turn to **264**.

3

River listens intensely as you explain the various theories flying around on why her and Tim might be plausible Traitors.

'Wow,' she says. 'I didn't see that one coming. I mean, after last night, Tim, sure. But why are they looking at me suddenly? I hope I can count on you later if it comes down to it.' You nod, wondering all the time what you will do.

River excuses herself and says she needs to go and get changed before Round Table. You have ten blissful minutes as you sit with your eyes closed, listening to the tick of a clock, before Gabriel puts his head around the door and says, 'It's time.'

You get up and walk towards the Round Table.

- Turn to **176**.

When you arrive, you say hello to a few people, sharing the odd joke, trying to project confidence.

'Remember, you are yet to banish a Traitor,' says your Host. 'If even one of them remains at the end, they will win.'

There is a pause, then Gregg clears his throat. Whenever you're around Gregg at the moment, you get pretty apprehensive.

What do you do?

- Jump in before Gregg can start speaking. Turn to **83**.

- Let Gregg speak, making sure you don't look like you're fearful of what he has to say. Turn to **61**.

DAY 10

As you walk downstairs, all you can think is 'walk like a Faithful, walk like a Faithful.' You're the first one in for breakfast this morning and you wonder if it's been done to put more pressure on you. You concentrate on the basics of a Faithful-looking breakfast. Not a phrase you ever thought you'd use. After all, for the Faithfuls, the big news is that Nina was banished. You have to remember that.

Suddenly it hits you that you only have to stay for another couple of days and you're in with a very good chance of winning.

However, right now, you can barely work out if you want toast or half a grapefruit.

The first knock at the door is Gregg. He looks as if he hasn't slept all night. Even though Nina had been a Traitor, she was a beloved part of the group and it's clearly hit him hard.

'Hooray,' he says, smiling ruefully. 'It's me.'

You smile genuinely. 'I'm not sure I have a hooray in me this morning, I'm afraid,' you say.

There's another knock and Gabriel puts his head around the door, then Anna, then River, then Ruby, all with the same subdued sense of celebration, as people shuffle about fixing themselves coffee. You realise suddenly how much of a threat Ruby is, now you're not on the same side.

Then the room realises that it's only Tim and Precious who aren't there. You make a conscious effort to go along with the muttering.

There's a gentle knock on the door . . . and Tim comes around the corner, smiling. He scans the room and quickly works out who is missing. 'Oh, no . . .' But then there is a knock at the door and Precious enters, smiling. The room erupts into cheers. River runs to hug her. Tim holds his heart. They really are very good at this.

'Well, I'm sorry, Precious, but last time this happened they recruited another Traitor,' says Gabriel. 'I'm happy to see you. But I can't help but feel a bit worried what this means too.'

'It is a bit unsettling, isn't it?' agrees Tim, sipping a cup of tea.

After breakfast, Gregg tells everyone he's going for a walk and sets off on his own. The others pair off: River, Precious and Ruby to sit on the steps and Gabriel, Tim and Anna to the library.

What do you do?

- Catch up with River, Precious and Ruby. Turn to **125**.

- Go with Gabriel, Tim and Anna. Turn to **68**.

6

As you cross the room, you spot Deb sitting on her own looking visibly upset.

'I just feel so bad, you know,' she says. 'I was so sure last night, but I was wrong.'

Her eyes are genuinely shining with tears, but again, you can't help but wonder if it might be a strategy. If she is a Traitor and has the spotlight on her, wouldn't this be the exact right way to play things?

You pat her arm, make some sympathetic noises and move along.

- Turn to **30**.

7

Tim stands over by the window and watches Gregg walking across the lawn in the distance. 'Well, there's a Traitor-hunter with the weight of the world on his shoulders,' he says. 'I should really go and talk to him.'

'I'm not sure if looking sad because you've banished a Traitor would be my strategy,' says Anna. 'If I was advising his life insurer, I'd say there was some extra risk there!'

You realise that might be the first time you've heard Anna make a joke.

'The way I see it, Gregg's behaviour makes sense as one of two options,' says Anna. 'Either he is genuinely shocked by the news that Nina was a Traitor. Or he's a Traitor who threw Nina under the bus and feels guilty.'

You nod along. It's certainly an interesting choice of behaviour from Gregg. Which makes you wonder if it isn't genuine after all.

'I would never argue with you on strategy, Anna,' says Tim, 'but I have a question. Do you feel as confident making predictions about the people who just keep themselves to themselves?'

'Like who?'

He pauses. 'Like Ruby, say? Or Precious?' As ever with Tim, it's said with a very breezy tone, but there's something forceful about it. 'Or perhaps it's just that I've never liked "Ruby Tuesday" as a song.' He has his eyes closed but you see the others looking at him a little bemused.

'Well, there's certainly less data to go on,' concedes Anna. 'If she is a Traitor, then her question about whether anyone has changed their behaviour was very clever. Because it made her seem like she was rooting out Traitors, but, of course, we don't know her, so can't judge if *her* behaviour has changed. Precious is even more of a mystery as she's taken much more of a back seat. It's just the sort of devious thing to happen in this place for them to send in a Traitor.'

Tim sips from his tea, looking thoughtful. You chat for a while and then decide it's time for a change of scene.

- Turn to **32**.

8

You go and sit next to River, who thinks that Jorge is a big loss.

'Anna's kept a record of who's voted for who at Round Table. Apparently Jorge has the best record on not voting for Traitors.'

'Had,' you remark. A thought occurs: 'Listen, have you talked to Nina about . . . you know?'

'Grannygate?' asks River, with a look.

'Stop it,' you say.

'Yeah, me and Nina were the first ones down. She didn't actually seem massively cut up about it. Which is a bit weird, right? Her own granddaughter, a Faithful, getting kicked out?'

River might be onto something, you think, but on the other hand, you've got to try and stay in the game whether you're a murderous visitor to the Conclave or a tried and true Faithful.

- Turn to **180**.

9

You make your excuses and explain you've already agreed to meet someone, hoping it doesn't appear too obvious that you're avoiding a conversation with them. You wander in the garden, enjoying being on your own for a while. As you come round a corner, you bump into Nina and Rakayah. Rakayah says she's going to go back to the Castle, but Nina joins you out under the trees. She points out a couple of plants and you look politely.

'Lovely girl, but very young,' she says, as she watches Rakayah in the distance. 'She keeps telling me she thinks I'm *marvellous*. I remember when seventy seemed a very long way away.'

You smile and look down. Then you suggest it's time to head inside. You bump into Teddy, who says, 'It's Round Table time.'

- Turn to **141**.

10

'You're right, Teddy, I wasn't being honest with you,' you say.

'I knew it!' he shouts.

'But the reason I couldn't meet your eye isn't that I'm a Traitor. It's just that I was worried I'd laugh. Because, if I'm honest, this feels a bit silly to me.' You look around the table, meeting people's eyes. 'I'm going to be completely honest now. I have no idea who is a Traitor. No grand plan. No big theory. I might as well flip a coin. All I know is that I'm a Faithful.'

Your Host announces, 'Faithfuls and Traitors, it is time to carry out your first banishment. Please write down who you think should leave the game.'

Suddenly it all seems very real. In a few moments' time, someone will leave the room, and the game, for good. You ask yourself who's acting most like a Traitor, and while of course any of you could be innocent, Steve-O is the one who seems most defensive.

As those ahead of you read out the name they've written down, almost everyone has written Steve-O. When it's your turn to justify it, you just say, 'I had to write someone, I'm sorry.'

River and Laure actually vote for Tim but, other than that, it's time for Steve-O to leave. It's a big moment, watching him stand. His upper lip is trembling.

'Steve-O,' intones your Host. 'You have been banished. Before you leave the Castle, it's time to reveal whether you're Faithful or a Traitor.'

'I'd just like to say,' offers Steve-O, 'I honestly thought I'd be here longer than this. I wasn't sure I'd win, but this . . .' He peters out. 'You messed up, guys. I'm a Faithful. Or was.'

'Oh Jesus!' barks Rakayah.

'This is on me, guys, I'm sorry, I rushed things,' offers Irwin. 'Steve-O, you're right, I'm so sorry, mate.'

YOU HAVE BANISHED A FAITHFUL.

- Turn to **69**.

11

'If I may,' you say. 'I have always tried to play things by my head. But now I'd like to appeal from the heart. I am a Faithful. I know that to be true.' As you speak, you look around and make eye contact with every one of them. 'I hope that my behaviour in here has earned me your trust. I haven't got everything right, no one has, but I've acted like a Faithful from day one. However, whatever happens, I don't think it's right for any of us to not face the same scrutiny. River, you have always been great at summing up the mood of the group, but I don't think now is the time for that. You should face the same scrutiny as the rest of us. There's just something about how eager you are to control what we all think.' Ruby nods vigorously. But Gabriel looks uncomfortable that you have been so aggressive.

All too soon, it's time. But this time you are collected and taken down to the front of the Castle. In the shadows you think you must be where you had first stood on the grass what seems like a lifetime ago. Your Host steps forwards.

- Turn to **25**.

While you wait to be called in, a few people open a pack of cards and you decide to join in.

BONUS GAME

CAPTURE THE CASTLE: JESTER

You need: deck of cards, phone with timer

Players: Town Crier, plus at least two others

Take from the deck two 2s (the Renegades) and one joker (the Court Jester). Then add court cards (king, queen, jack) until there are three more cards than there are players.

One player is the Town Crier and should now read the text below.

I am shuffling the cards, and dealing one to everyone, including myself.

I am now placing the remaining cards face down in a row on the table.

Everyone, look at your card. If you have a 2, you are a Renegade, come to capture the castle. If you have a joker, you are the Court Jester. Everyone else is a member of the Royal

Family. Place your card face down, close to the three already on the table in a way that makes it clear whose is whose.

When I say, 'Let us dance!', the Masked Ball will commence. Everyone – including me – will close their eyes for a count of eight. During that time, any Renegades must open their eyes and clock each other.

Ready . . . Let us dance! One, two, three, four, five, six, seven . . . eight.

Everyone must open their eyes. When I say, 'Send for the Jester!', we will all again close our eyes for a count of eight. During that time, the Court Jester may silently swap, without turning them over, any two cards, or may choose not to.

Ready . . . Send for the Jester! One, two, three, four, five, six, seven . . . eight.

Everyone must open their eyes. The King has heard that there may be a Renegade at his Masked Ball. In five minutes' time, he will have someone put in the stocks.

Your identity is the one on the card in your place, regardless of what you started with. You have five minutes to debate whom to put in the stocks. Any of you may claim to have been assigned any of the identities – Royal Family, Renegade or Jester.

The time starts . . . now.

Set the timer, and then when the time is up . . .

After a count of five, we shall all vote. The player or players with the most votes shall be placed in the stocks.

If one or more Renegades is placed in the stocks, the Royal Family shall be declared victorious. If there were no

Renegades, the Royal Family shall be declared victorious. In all other situations, the Renegades shall be declared victorious. If you decide that the King should exhibit clemency, you should now agree to each vote for the player on your left, and nobody shall be placed in the stocks.

I shall now make the count of five. One, two, three, four, five.

NB: this game can be combined with other Capture the Castle games in the list of games at the start of the book, so long as the total number of cards is always topped up to three more than the number of players using members of the Royal Family.

Just as you finish the game, you hear your name being called and it's time for you to meet your Host.

- Turn to **290**.

13

'I wouldn't have ever thought it in a million years till last night,' you say. 'She's a total Faithful. But then Nina? I'm not saying I'm totally agreeing with you at all. But I'm not ruling it out either.'

'Ooh, careful with those splinters in your bum from sitting on that fence!' says Ruby. You can't help but warm to her. She's forthright and charming. All the qualities you'd need to be a brilliant Traitor, you immediately think.

'Let's both just keep an eye on River then,' she says. And you nod.

'Right. We should go join up with the others,' Ruby says. 'Before they start to gossip!'

As you head into the corridor, your Host addresses you from the stairs.

'Right, time for you to join together, Faithfuls and Traitors, and complete today's Mission.'

- Turn to **252**.

14

'You know, Gabriel, until a few nights ago, not in a million years,' you say. 'Then Nina happened. I'm not saying I'm totally agreeing on River. But I'm not ruling it out either.'

You feel proud of your reasoning. River was right, the trick is just to pretend you don't know that you're a Traitor.

'That's exactly how I feel,' says Gabriel. 'Let's both just keep an eye on her.'

You nod.

Then word comes around that it's time for the Mission.

- Turn to **252**.

15

When it is your turn to speak, you address River. 'River, I didn't mean to attack you back there. But it came from passion because I know I am a Faithful. Like you. And we have to act as a team.'

You spend so much time addressing your comments to her that you don't leave yourself enough time for Gabriel. And River is refusing to meet your eye. When she speaks, she addresses mainly Ruby and lays out passionately why she so often feels herself speaking for the group. Because she is so passionately a Faithful. You realise that you have misjudged things.

'Now it is time for you to vote again,' says your Host.

This time, you write River. Ruby changes her mind and votes for you. River has written your name. Gabriel again votes for you.

You step forwards. And your Host asks you to say if you are Faithful or a Traitor. You stand before them, your heart beating so loudly you think they must be able to hear it. You wish you could tell them that you weren't always a Traitor, how hard it was to lie to them, even for this amount of time, but you can't.

All you can say is:

'I am a Traitor.'

There is a gasp and then a cheer.

YOU HAVE BEEN BANISHED.

To play this day again, please turn to **267**. Better luck next time!

16

'Hmmm, I'm not getting the vibes that anyone is massively into Gregg. We might have to think again.' You keep your face studiously blank. This is exactly the sort of thing that could drag you into the spotlight tonight. Team Traitor loyalty is one thing, but you need to keep River in the dark as far as possible.

Thankfully Ruby comes out and says, 'Last game in the library before tonight?' And you both head back inside.

- Turn to **288**.

As if to undermine the seriousness of what is to come, it's a beautiful morning and you catch up with River and Ruby as they're heading down the steps towards one of the walled gardens.

'We thought we'd better make the most of it, as any one of us could be leaving in a few hours,' says River. You walk along a gravel path and through into a redbrick garden with neat rows of vegetables and herbs. Bees fly lazily in between plants.

'Well, come on then,' says River to Ruby. 'You always have a working theory.' Your pulse immediately quickens.

'I've got nothing,' says Ruby. 'My plan has been to watch everyone's reaction really carefully at the last couple of banishments, to see if there was anything unusual that was a clue. But they're such emotional events, it's really hard to know what the normal way to react is.'

'That's so true,' says River. 'It's like at school when the teacher would say whoever did the thing needs to own up, and even though you know you didn't do it, you feel like you're acting guiltily. I one hundred per cent know I'm Faithful, but I'm still there second-guessing my reactions.' You can't get over how naturally she lies. It's either impressive or terrifying, you can't decide.

'I feel like we constantly find a frame that explains behaviour as odd or suspicious,' you say. 'But it's actually just that this is a fundamentally odd situation.'

As you walk past strawberry plants under a net, you think back to the last couple of banishments. What clues might there have been? Had you left any?

As you reach the other side of the garden, you explain you're going to head back inside and they wave you away.

- Turn to **287**.

18

You arrive downstairs first. Breakfast is the quietest it's ever been, which is useful because you realise you are again second-guessing everything. Is this the way a Faithful would stir sugar into their coffee? Is this more of a Traitor's way of dipping a soldier into a boiled egg? It's ten minutes in and you have no idea how River and Tim have done it.

One by one, the knock at the door and then the wave and the smile: Gregg, Gabriel, River and Tim. You have to make a conscious effort not to search out Tim and River for a reassuring glance. And you suddenly realise you should have been paying attention to who wasn't making eye contact in the mornings.

Then you all realise it's between Precious and Ruby. You have to remind yourself that you don't 'know' it's Precious. Then the knock at the door, and Ruby pokes her head around the door. She is smiling, but then immediately her face drops when she realises that Precious has been murdered.

There is a babble of conversation. River goes over and squeezes Ruby's arm.

You end up sitting with Tim and Gabriel and make some chitchat, mainly about how intense the previous night was.

'Who's going to make me my tea now?' says Tim. 'Anna was the only one who made it strong enough.' Gabriel nods and smiles. You laugh too but worry it was overly loud. A Traitorous laugh.

River pipes up, 'Cheer up everyone. Last night was rough but we're nearly there!' A couple of people raise their cups and give a muted cheer.

As you're all leaving, you think you see a gesture from Ruby. If you had to translate it into words, it would be something like, 'Would you hang back?' Your heart starts beating quickly. Is she on to you?

What do you do?

- Wait for Ruby. Turn to **255**.

- Leave with everyone else. Turn to **169**.

19

After the Mission, where you were finally part of the winning team, you, Ruby and Gregg head to the Armoury. You walk down a long corridor to a cool, dark room full of suits of armour and glass cabinets containing long, sharp things. You enter the private chamber and are faced with the numbered chests. For no particular reason, you pick chest three, only to find it empty. But unless either or both Ruby and Gregg are a Traitor, just getting to the room means you can relax somewhat. As you all head back from the Armoury, you hang back a bit so it's just you and Gregg.

'Weird one last night?' you say.

He nods. 'It's weird because I should be really happy. But I never thought Nina was a Traitor, I was just genuinely confused by the florist thing. And now I feel like I don't know anything. I'm half hoping I get banished tonight, to be honest. I'm not sure I've got it in me any more.' He seems so down that you have to say something.

'Oh, don't say that,' you say. 'It's all part of the game, isn't it?'

Gregg sighs. 'I know, and that's what Tim has been saying to me, trying to make me feel better. I just know that everyone is off gossiping about me and I feel like I have this massive target on my back.'

What do you do?

- Be honest and say that people were a little taken aback by the way he's been behaving. Turn to **248**.

- Try not to stress him out and say there's not a problem. Turn to **93**.

20

You sit quietly, and into the gap Ruby speaks eloquently and passionately about why she is Faithful. But she also lets River have it for trying to guide the room again, which she says is a big red flag for her.

You try and stay neutral but find yourself nodding vigorously and Gabriel is looking at both of you a little strangely. Perhaps this confrontation has been too much for someone as finely tuned to pleasantry as him.

All too soon, it's time. But this time you are collected and taken down to the front of the Castle. In the shadows you think you must be where you had first stood on the grass what seems like a lifetime ago. Your Host steps forwards.

- Turn to **210**.

21

At the end, the screens are removed. But something has changed. There's one more table than when you started.

Sitting at it are two people (both with sauce on their chins).

And then you realise that you recognise them.

A loud cheer goes up: it's Precious and Ruby! So they weren't eliminated after all?

'As you know,' your Host explains, 'in The Traitors, there are only two ways of leaving the Castle. Murder and banishment. So these two players never left. They've been waiting to come back.'

They're definitely both Faithfuls, you think to yourself. Then you catch yourself. Do you *really* know that? Wouldn't it be just like this place to throw you another curve ball?

Other players seem to be taking a moment to process the information, then River lets out another cheer and everyone joins in. This is an unambiguously happy moment. Then it's time for the winners to take a trip to the Armoury while the rest of you look on with envy. Though you tried your hardest, you weren't part of the winning group.

- Turn to **95**.

Deep breath, you're doing this. When it is your turn to speak, you address Gabriel. 'Gabriel, I know you thought I was aggressive back there, and I know someone like you doesn't respond well to that. But I swear to you that it comes from passion. I am a Faithful. You know that River has always been there, guiding what we do. Deep down, you know that River is a Traitor.'

River gives you a studiously calm look and defends herself by attacking you. But it can't help but feel like revenge and you can see Gabriel looking at her thoughtfully as she speaks.

'Now it is time for you to vote again,' says your Host.

This time, you write River. Ruby writes River. River has written your name. Gabriel has changed his mind and written River's name.

'River, you have been banished. Please tell us if you are Faithful or a Traitor.'

She steps forwards. 'I am a Traitor.'

There is a mood of celebration and Gabriel and Ruby can't help but smile.

'So,' says your Host. 'The final three. Please step forwards and reveal whether you are Faithful or a Traitor.'

Gabriel steps forwards, smiling. 'When I came in here, I knew I just wanted to be me, whatever else happened. I wanted to be true to myself. And that's why I'm so happy to say that I am a Faithful.'

Ruby steps forwards and pauses. 'I might have rejoined the game late, but I am so thrilled to be able to say with all my heart that I am a Faithful.'

As you stand in front of them, your heart beating so loudly you think they must be able to hear it, part of you wishes you could tell them that you weren't always a Traitor; how hard it had been to lie to them, even for this small amount of time, but then you realise what this means. You can't help but smile. 'Sorry, I'm a Traitor.'

YOU HAVE WON.

23

'Well, Gregg, I'm pretty sure there are some people who think this is how a Traitor might act if they'd taken out one of their own. But I would say there's an equally strong school of thought that you're just upset like all of us that Nina was a Traitor.' He looks at you and even that small moment of kindness seems to have rejuvenated him.

'Thank you for your honesty,' he says. If only he knew, you think.

Up ahead, Gabriel calls back, 'Everyone's going to play a game in the library!' You both quicken your pace to catch up with the others.

- Turn to **240**.

MISSION

GUEST OF HONOUR

You need: pencil and paper, phone with timer

Players: Host, plus at least three others

Before the game begins, the Host creates slips of paper and writes the same name (a real or fictional person) – the Guest of Honour – on all but one of them. The remaining slip must read 'Gatecrasher'.

The slips are folded over, shuffled and distributed. The timer is set to go off after seven minutes (or a duration chosen by the Host).

The Host picks one player and asks them a question about the Guest of Honour. For example: 'Is the Guest of Honour a witty person?'

That person answers (bluffing, if they're the Gatecrasher), then chooses a different player and asks them another question.

The Gatecrasher tries to use the information to infer the identity of the Guest of Honour. The other players try to work out the identity of the Gatecrasher.

At any moment, one player can accuse another of being the Gatecrasher. If anyone other than the accused disagrees, the accusation is immediately dropped and play continues from where it left off.

Also at any moment, the Gatecrasher can reveal their identity. They then have one chance to guess the name of the Guest of Honour.

Here are the ways that the game can end:

- *A unanimous accusation correctly identifies the Gatecrasher (who is the loser)*

- *A unanimous accusation turns out to be wrong (and the Gatecrasher wins)*

- *The Gatecrasher correctly identifies the Guest of Honour (and wins)*

- *The Gatecrasher makes an inaccurate guess (and loses)*

- *The time runs out (and the Gatecrasher wins)*

Then play again with a new Guest of Honour.

- Turn to **311**.

'Now,' says your Host. 'This is where things get really intense. If you are absolutely confident that all of you are Faithfuls, then we can stop the game now. But remember, if there is a Traitor here, then they have won. So, if you wish, you can make the decision to banish one further person. Which will you choose?' Your Host gestures for you to look next to you. 'Beside you is a chest with two ceremonial pouches in it. One is labelled "End Game". The other "Banish Again". When you have made your decision, hand over your chosen pouch and we will reveal your decision.'

Your head is spinning. You hadn't thought properly about what might happen. But of course there is one final twist. Things are getting very serious. You look around you. Ruby is frowning and looking at River. Gabriel looks serene.

At the last moment, you grab the 'Banish Again' pouch and hand it over.

'First, River,' says your Host. The pouch is thrown into the fire and green smoke rises. *End Game.*

'Now, Gabriel,' says your Host. Another pouch and green smoke, curling up into the night sky, lit by the flames. *End Game.*

When your pouch goes into the fire, the smoke is red, swirling around you. *Banish Again.*

'Now, Ruby,' says your Host. Appropriately, the smoke is lit ruby. *Banish Again.*

'So,' your Host says. 'You're not sure. Time to take your slates and write the name of who you will now, finally, banish.'

What do you do?

- Write Gabriel. Turn to **135**.

- Write River. Turn to **99**.

- Write Ruby. Turn to **215**.

26

In the library it's dark and cool. For a moment, you wonder who has read the books that line the shelves. You slip into an armchair as a conversation has already started.

'Forgive me for piloting, so to speak,' says Irwin. 'Old habits. But what do we all think is going on?'

'I think he was a safe choice,' says Gregg (Salford, 29). 'Stands to reason. If you're a murderer. Pick someone who isn't one of the leaders for the first murder.'

'Oh, that's devious,' says Gabriel (Anglesey, 43). 'I could never think like that.' You wonder for a moment if anyone is really as nice as he appears to be.

Teddy is clearly chafing at the bit. 'It's classic game theory, isn't it, man. You pick someone with no clear reason and then watch as everyone tries to solve it. Then you shake loose who the real threats are. It's like crypto . . .'

- Turn to **101**.

Isla is with River, Gregg and Deb. Deb is deep in a conversation about body language. 'I was interested in how you'd respond this morning, Isla, poor you, 'cause I've seen the signs of shock; you see them all the time in the courtroom, like every day.'

She says it's 'one of the basic primal reactions' and claims that it's impossible to 'act' shocked; for the eyebrows to go that high if a person isn't genuinely shocked.

You're not one hundred per cent sure she knows what she's talking about.

'That's why I can't really enjoy some kinds of movies. You see the acting and it doesn't look right. When you know, you know – you know? That's why I prefer comedies.'

Isla tries to get back to the topic: 'So are you saying I was shocked this morning? Or acting?'

'Neither, actually,' reckons Deb.

'That's probably because I wasn't shocked.'

'Wait, what?' asks River. 'I was shocked, and I wasn't even BFFs with Amrit like you were.'

'Yeah, but we'd been talking a lot about how it could be anyone. We'd joke: see you tomorrow, if you're still here, kind of thing. Literally the morning before he was murdered, he told me they were going to go after a good egg.'

As they carry on discussing whether or not Amrit's murder should have been a surprise, Gregg whispers to you jovially, 'I'm a bit of a body language reader myself sometimes. Finding Laure absolutely scintillating at breakfast, were you?'

This worries you. You don't want the others being able to read when you're not feeling like the loyal team player the name 'Faithful' suggests.

'Don't worry, she couldn't tell. I could see that. Like I say, just an amateur body language reader. Not a pro like Deb, of course.'

You wonder to yourself: is Gregg deliberately being snide? Or is he trying to be funny but it's just not coming across very well? He has a kind of pleasant, open demeanour and you had assumed he was basically a simple bloke, but now you're not so sure.

- Turn to **120**.

28

'Leaving aside the fact that I didn't actually know what the secret was, just that there was a secret, I think we're getting distracted from the main point here, which is that Nina has been lying to us the entire time. On top of what happened with Deb, it's just too much. If that isn't the marker of a Traitor, I don't know what is. And if you knew you were lying, why would you draw attention to it by going on about plants so much!'

Nina was already annoyed at Gregg and this double attack only makes her more so. She tries to argue against both of you, but her anger makes her clumsy and it ends up diluting both of her attacks. She forgets to defend her original lie.

Then Tim and River sadly and regretfully say they feel let down by her. Anna agrees and things are set.

As the names are revealed, it's looking pretty even between you,

Gregg and Nina. But as River and Tim both hold up Nina's name one after the other, it's her by one vote. Precious is shaking her head and muttering that there's something off here but you barely take it in.

As your Host brings Nina forwards to tell the room if she's Faithful or a Traitor, there is still a tremor of emotion in her voice.

'Well, since we're being honest . . . I'm a Traitor.'

The room erupts with excited chatter. Gregg looks sad but relieved to be staying. Tim just looks shocked.

YOU HAVE BANISHED A TRAITOR.

- Turn to **58**.

29

You follow the sound of voices and slip quietly into a garden chair as Steve-O holds forth.

'All I'm saying is, when you're a coastguard, there are some people you meet that you'd have in your boat, and some people you wouldn't, right?'

Isla is watching very intently and nodding. You check to see if anyone else has noticed, and then worry you're doing exactly the same thing.

'You're absolutely right, mate,' says David (Henley-upon-Thames, 49), nodding vigorously. 'It's the same in the pub game. There are people you want beside you on a Saturday night rush when there's no salt and vinegar and a barrel needs changing. And people you don't. Luke was a lovely feller but he wasn't Saturday night material.'

You can't quite follow the logic of the argument, never mind the idea that pulling pints and saving lives are the same thing, and you are going to say something when Alexis (Edinburgh, 39) pipes up.

'So you're saying they got rid of him to help us?'

'Eh?' says Steve-O.

'Well, if he was such a bad teammate, why did the Traitors murder him? They're hardly going to help us, are they?'

'Well, at breakfast, Elif was saying her theory is they got rid of him because no one is *that* bad at names.' You can hear the wheels turning in everyone's heads as they think about that.

- Turn to **123**.

30

As you make for the main doors to go and get some air you encounter Nina, who looks pretty miserable too. Even walking in the gardens hasn't cheered her up this morning.

'Tough one last night, wasn't it?' you say.

She nods. 'I just feel sorry for Deb, you know.'

You nod, interested that they had clearly become so close.

'Well, for Isla and Amrit too, obviously,' she says quickly. 'But it messes with your head, doesn't it? I heard over breakfast that you had an argument with Laure.'

'Who said that?!' you ask.

'Oh, I think Gregg and Rakayah were discussing it.'

You suggest you both return to the Castle.

- Turn to **251**.

31

DAY 4

You and River are the first ones in the breakfast room. Neither of you has much of an appetite, as you half-heartedly scrape some jam on your toast. You notice that there's barely a person that arrives without River saying some version of 'Yes, I thought they'd be safe' and nodding wisely to herself. Though you notice that she doesn't do it for Skye and Laure and wonder idly if that means something significant, or whether perhaps she just doesn't like them.

In any event, everyone arrives except Alexis, Jorge and Nina . . . until Jorge and Nina come through the door. There are cheers for them, but they are very quick to scan the room and splutter: 'So it's Alexis!'

'It's Alexis!' confirms Rakayah. 'Oh, poor Alexis! I . . . I . . . poor Alexis!'

You are thinking the same thing, but not quite as . . . intensely. Indeed, you can't help but feel that in many ways Alexis has taken a bullet that could have been meant for you.

You wonder: is Rakayah really in shock – her eyes look genuinely teary to you – or is she hiding something? If you were a Traitor, then being overly shocked and emotional when someone was murdered would be a smart way of deflecting suspicion. But after yesterday, do you really want to be visibly coming up with more theories, or keeping your head down?

What do you do?

- Take Rakayah at face value and console her? Turn to **111**.

- Share your doubts about her with Gabriel? Turn to **138**.

32

You head outside to see what the weather is doing and almost don't notice River, who is laid on her back on one of the steps.

'Ooh, you snuck up on me,' she says. 'Sorry, I got no sleep last night.' She sits up and looks at you. 'What's the vibe in there?'

'Hmmm, no real insight. Tim is looking at Ruby and Precious and whether they'd send a Traitor in like that. I think the consensus is that we'd put nothing past them.'

'Is he?' says River, looking thoughtful. 'And that's very interesting in relation to what Ruby just said. That maybe we need to start thinking about Anna and Tim as the ultimate camouflaged Traitors.'

Your expression must have given you away because she laughs. 'I know, the vending machine. It's all any of us can talk about.'

'I know,' you say. 'Laughter was my initial reaction. But it has made me realise. They're the only two of us who haven't really ever faced serious scrutiny. Especially Anna. It feels wrong, but maybe that's what it would feel like if you were an amazing Traitor?'

'Or that's what Ruby wants us to start thinking if *she's* an amazing Traitor,' you say.

River just lays back down. A couple of minutes later word comes round that it's time for the day's Mission.

- Turn to **228**.

33

'Yeah, you're probably right,' he replies, sotto voce. 'I just need to find the right moment.'

That was easier than it might have been, you think to yourself. You smile and continue along the landing. Coming up the stairs is Gabriel. You wonder how much he heard. You smile at him too and he beckons you in for a word.

'What were you and Gregg whispering about?' he asks. 'Cloak-and-dagger stuff?' He's smiling, but from bitter experience you know how things can escalate and you want to make sure you get this right.

What do you do?

- Tell him that Gregg wanted to share a theory about someone. Turn to **175**.

- Make up some dull answer to end the conversation. Turn to **272**.

34

When you get back inside, you head to the library, where Gabriel is playing Patience on his own. You stand and watch him for a moment. 'Any luck yet?' you ask. He sighs and puts the cards down. 'My head's not in the game.'

'Yes, I think we all feel a bit like that today,' you say. 'So what's the word on the street?'

'Well, we're slightly torn over Gregg as supremely sensitive or Traitor. And Tim seems *really* quite keen on Ruby or Precious as a potential Traitor now, because they both played their first Round Table brilliantly and there's now a thought that perhaps that's exactly what a smart Traitor would have done. Or not.'

'Very interesting,' you say. 'Especially as Ruby was just hypothesising that Tim and Anna would make sense as the last Traitors you'd ever suspect.'

Gabriel pulls a face but becomes calmer. 'God, that speech from Anna last night about vending machines. She was giddy, wasn't she? Actually, Tim or her isn't *impossible*, is it?' he says. 'Last time we voted out the last person any of us had suspected, she was a Traitor.' You just shrug. 'OK,' says Gabriel. 'How about a game of Snap?' But luckily you're saved as word comes round that it's time for the day's Mission.

- Turn to **228**.

35

'I wouldn't have ever suspected River in a million years till a couple of nights ago,' you say. 'Then Nina happened. I'm not saying I'm totally agreeing with you at all. But I'm not ruling it out either.' You feel proud of your reasoning. River was right, the trick is just to pretend you don't know that you're a Traitor.

'Ooh, careful with those splinters in your bum from sitting on that fence!' says Ruby. You can't help but warm to her. She's forthright and charming. But dangerously sharp. You can see why you couldn't murder her, but you wish she wasn't in the game.

'Let's both just keep an eye on River,' she says. And you nod.

'Right. We should go join up with the others,' Ruby says. 'Before they start to gossip!'

Then word comes around that it's time for the Mission.

- Turn to **252**.

Some people decide to take their hot drinks with them and play a game in the library and you tag along. After all, it's a great way to learn people's names!

BONUS GAME

THE WIDE THRONE

You need: pencil and paper; as many chairs as players, plus one more

Players: an even number, eight or more

Four of the chairs should be placed in a row (a sofa seating four can do the same job). This is the Wide Throne. The other chairs form an arc from one end of the Wide Throne to the other.

Players are divided into two teams of equal size: children versus adults or any arbitrary allocation of your choice. (For example, players with hats versus hatless players.)

Each player writes their name on a piece of paper. These

are mixed up and handed back out: players secretly read their name (it's OK if you get your own name).

Players now sit in an arrangement that alternates the teams (child, adult, child, adult, etc.), with all four spots on the Wide Throne occupied and one empty space.

The object of the game is to be the first team to occupy all four spots on the Wide Throne.

The player to the left of the Wide Throne says the name of any player. The player who is holding the paper with that name moves to the empty space. Those two players then swap their pieces of paper.

Play continues with the player to the right of the new empty spot giving another name.

Players use memory and strategy to manoeuvre four of their team on to the Wide Throne.

After the game, you spill out into the hallway, people already beginning to separate into groups and whispering their theories to each other.

People are clearly watching each other intently for their reaction to everything, and you are slightly spooked and worried that you somehow got the reaction to the first murder 'wrong'. It wouldn't do to get a reputation this early on. After all, at this stage, this is basically a popularity contest.

It's time to try and meet some new people. From what you can see, there are at least three groups to choose from.

What do you do?

- Head outside to the garden with a group headed up by Steve-O. Turn to **29**.

- Head into the library with a group headed up by Irwin. Turn to **26**.

- Head to the drawing room with a group headed up by Rakayah. Turn to **282**.

37

'I was just saying the same thing earlier,' you say. 'And I'd almost forgotten the stuff with Deb before that. But it feels like Gregg's had a real run of dramas, hasn't he? But equally, I don't think it's beyond possibility that it's down to his . . . lack of subtlety around certain things? I think there's definitely an angle that works for us tonight if we want to use it.'

River is nodding along. 'Oh, that's true for sure. You'll never get poor betting on a man's capacity to read a situation wrong!'

Ruby comes out and says, 'Last game in the library before tonight?' And you both head back inside.

- Turn to **288**.

38

Later, once everyone's had a well-earned rest, a group are sitting in the bar.

Amrit's main concern, when discussing the activity, is that if he'd known it was going to be so strenuous, he wouldn't have worn one of his 'more dapper shirts'. It has been remarked upon a few times that Amrit seems to own exclusively patterned shirts of a very specific sort.

This causes widespread – fond – amusement, with Isla remarking, 'One of these days you'll have to show us what you think an un-dapper shirt looks like.'

'You need a mind like Anna's to work out stuff like that river crossing,' Rakayah observes.

'Mind like Anna's,' echoes Deb.

'Well, we're certainly getting to know how people think,' observes Amrit. You don't think he means much by it, so you're surprised by Rakayah's response:

'Sorry, what do you mean by that?'

Amrit looks a little at sea, too.

'Like, a couple of days ago we didn't know each other. It's amazing how quickly you can get to know a person.'

'Or think you do,' replies Rakayah. 'First appearances can be deceptive.'

We're kind of past first impressions, though, you think to yourself. And need to be. There's a Round Table every day, after all. As if you've summoned it by thinking about it, people are calling out it's time for Round Table.

- Turn to **239**.

39

'I heard it too,' you say. 'But I didn't want to tell tales behind anyone's back, so I kept it to myself. I'm sorry to anyone who feels that was wrong. I just wasn't sure enough about what I'd heard to spread rumours.'

That seems to nip things in the bud. From this point onwards the conversation shifts back to Deb and Nina. It's clear that they are both well liked and there is genuine sympathy for Nina who keeps wiping at her eyes. But there is a real sense of betrayal in the room and Deb is bearing the brunt of it. She tries to mount a defence that she isn't a Traitor based on how stupid it would be to keep this a secret if she was. But it's almost as if the room doesn't really care. They just want revenge.

When it's time to pick names, it's pretty much unanimous for Deb. She accepts the news graciously, nodding her head once.

'And now,' the Host says, 'it's time to tell us, are you Faithful or a Traitor?'

'Well, I'm genuinely sorry that we lied to you. But I wasn't lying about one thing. I am a Faithful.'

Gregg bangs the table with his fist and swears. The rest of the room slumps back in silence, the only sound Nina quietly sobbing.

YOU HAVE BANISHED A FAITHFUL.

- Turn to **304**.

40

Look again, or count again. Is everyone where they should be? No. Return to **96** and try again.

41

'If I may,' you say. 'I have always tried to play things by my head. But now I'd like to appeal from the heart. I am Faithful. I know that to be true.' As you speak, you look around and make eye contact with every one of them. 'I hope that my behaviour in here has earned me your trust. But I fully understand if it hasn't. However, whatever happens, I don't think it's right for any of us to not face the same scrutiny. River, you have always been great at summing up the mood of the group, but I don't think now is the time for that. You should face the same scrutiny as the rest of us. There's just something about how eager you are to control what we all think.' Ruby nods vigorously. But Gabriel looks uncomfortable that you have been so aggressive.

All too soon, it's time. But this time you are collected and taken down to the front of the Castle. In the shadows you think you must be where you had first stood on the grass what seems like a lifetime ago. Your Host steps forwards.

- Turn to **62**.

'I've been speaking to a lot of people today,' you say, as you try and catch people's eyes, 'and we've all agreed that Steve-O has been really trying to lead the conversation. The more I think about it, the more I think that's exactly what a Traitor would do, if they were trying to control what everyone else was doing.' It sounds a bit vague, doesn't it? A little weak. You reach in your mind for some words that will motivate the room, or at least demotivate the room from ending your time in the Castle tonight.

'I just think we need to keep in mind that he's not the captain of this boat.' The words feel like the right ones as you say them. But immediately afterwards, they don't feel right at all. They feel mean. You didn't *mean* to sound mean, so to speak, but there's no doubt you sounded petty.

As you watch the looks on everyone's faces, you know it's going to come down to a vote between you and Tim and you honestly can't think of anyone you'd less like to be going up against; people seem to instantly take to Tim.

'Faithfuls and Traitors,' announces your Host, 'it is time to carry out your first banishment. Please write down who you think should leave the game.'

You write 'Steve-O', of course, but as the names come up, you discover not many others have. River has voted for Steve-O, and so has Laure. But that's it. All the others seem to have written down your name, and when the last vote is cast, your Host looks at you and says: 'You have been banished. Now, please tell us if you are Faithful or a Traitor.'

As you stand, ready to tell them that you're Faithful, it feels like no comfort at all.

YOU HAVE BEEN BANISHED.

To play this day again, please turn to **110**. Better luck next time!

43

In the hall, people are milling about. Apparently people are being called in one by one to meet with the Host. You find yourself standing next to Irwin (Carlisle, 41).

'Have you met Deb yet?' he asks?

You nod. 'She's very nice. Welsh.' At that moment, Amrit (Armagh, 29) and Isla (Isle of Man, 26) come past deep in conversation, though they nod to Irwin. 'Those two are firm friends already,' mutters Irwin. 'Who would have thought smelly oils were such a thing. He's one of those charity fundraisers. She owns one of those smelly-therapy shops. All very twenty-first century, isn't it?' You smile in a way that you hope implies neither approval nor disapproval, then make your apologies and move down the hall. Irwin is clearly a gossip and you're not sure you want to associate too visibly with him.

Further down the corridor, you are beckoned over by Steve-O (Lowestoft, 42), a coastguard. 'Come and meet these lovely people,' he says.

There's Rakayah. She's 'in IT'. Before you can say anything, she adds, 'I know that sounds really boring but, well, I mean, you'd probably find it boring. But I honestly don't.' This elicits an affectionate chuckle from Tim (Cornwall, 53), a park-keeper, who seems to be immediately playing the twinkly-eyed grandfather figure of the wider group, even though he's not actually that old.

- Turn to **12**.

44

'I'll go first this time,' you say. 'And it was actually something you said earlier, Ruby, that made me think of this.' She has a look of apprehension on her face. 'You said that it was hard to know what normal behaviour was in this environment. And that got me thinking about what is normal behaviour. And you know what isn't normal – one hundred per cent niceness all the time. Gabriel, you are either the nicest person in existence, or someone who has decided to craft a persona with only one note. A perfect Traitor.'

Gabriel is clearly shocked, and even hurt by your accusation. But he doesn't crumble. Instead he says that he has been utterly transparent and honest throughout the entire process. He says he is genuinely disappointed that you have attacked him like this after some of your conversations earlier, and concludes that the only reason for it must be that you are desperately trying to distract people from your own increasingly erratic behaviour. He says that tonight has made up his mind. You are a Traitor.

Ruby is also surprised by this sudden aggression on your part. River agrees that this feels like it bears little relationship to conversations you had earlier. So much for Team Traitor! Gregg says something vague about seeing everyone's point of view.

When the names are written, you vote for Gabriel, just for consistency as much as anything else, but everyone else votes for you. To come so close but so far from winning burns. You can't help but feel you played your cards poorly. No one remembers the name of the horse that falls at the final fence. You could kick yourself.

'I am . . . a Traitor,' you say.

YOU HAVE BEEN BANISHED.

To play this day again, please turn to **267**. Better luck next time!

'And then there were six,' says your Host. 'You have made it this far. But whose race is run? Tonight you must banish another. Let the games begin.'

There is a pause. And then Ruby lays out her suspicions about River and Tim. She's pretty even handed but River is clearly taken aback. She agrees that Tim makes sense to her but then clearly feels she needs to deflect even more and, as she looks around the room with the look of a drowning person searching for something that floats, her eyes alight upon you. She says that she's been getting funny vibes off you for a couple of days, like you've been keeping a secret. Oh dear.

Gabriel and Tim both agree that your behaviour has changed. Ruby is watching you intently. Even Gregg is looking at you strangely. Clearly they've noticed a change in you. You need to bring this back around or it's going to be all they talk about tonight.

What do you do?

- Tell them about the Traitors trying to seduce you the night before last. Turn to **221**.

- Come up with a different reason for your mood change. Turn to **146**.

You head outside to see what the weather is doing and almost don't notice River, who is laid on her back on one of the steps.

'Ooh, you snuck up on me,' she says. 'Sorry, I got no sleep last night.' She sits up and looks around. 'What's the vibe in there?' You desperately want to talk to her about how intense it is to be a Traitor, but you know you can't run the risk of saying anything overt and someone walking by.

'Hmmm, no real insight. Tim is looking at Ruby and Precious and whether they'd send a Traitor in like that. I think the consensus is that we'd put nothing past them. Not sure that's the best avenue to be honest. Should mention that to him.'

'Noted,' says River looking thoughtful. 'And that's very interesting in relation to what Ruby just said. That maybe we need to start thinking about Anna and Tim as the ultimate camouflaged Traitors.' She catches your eye. 'I obviously said that Anna makes more sense to me. But it's something for us to keep an eye on if we think there is a consensus on Tim.' It sounds so innocent but you think you know what she means.

It feels so nice, even if you can't actually trust them enough for there to be an 'us'. River lays back down with her eyes closed and you sit in companionable silence. A couple of minutes later word comes round that it's time for the day's Mission.

- Turn to **228**.

As you enter the drawing room, Anna is midway through a series of percentages and ratios and you can only assume that someone has made the mistake of asking her what it is an actuary actually does.

You're late to this, but everyone else looks as confused as you feel. 'But of course . . .' she's saying. I bet she says the thing about people again, you think.

'Being an actuary is actually about people, not numbers.' Bingo.

'I still don't get it,' remarks Gregg, confirming what you suspected. 'I mean, I think I'm more confused now than before I asked.'

'You know what, though, Gregg,' observes River, 'I've still got a better idea what Anna does for a living than I do you. You've not actually said.'

'I did, I told everyone on day one,' argues Gregg. 'I live in Salford and I work in the media.'

'Yeah, but so do I,' offers Teddy, 'and I've said what bit of the media. Podcasting. What about you?'

'Well, in my application I put "writer", and I mainly write crime fiction.'

'Crime?!?' repeats River. 'Is that allowed? I mean, you must know all about psychology and motivations and all that stuff?'

'Well, I suppose in a way, but it's not like I'm a criminologist or anything. It's really very different.'

A pause, then River says: 'I still think you should have just been honest with us, Gregg.'

'Well, now I wish I had!' replies Gregg. 'Can we just pretend I did?' He grins, and looks like he hopes his humour has defused anything that needed defusing.

If it was anyone else, you'd be worried for them, but Gregg seems bulletproof.

Someone shouts out to ask if anyone is up for a game of cards in the library and you wander over.

- Turn to **156**.

You arrive back as everyone is gathering out in front of the Castle. Your Host steps forwards.

'Well, Faithfuls and Traitors, it's time for you to again put your differences aside and work together in today's Mission.'

MISSION

ONYX

Players: four or more

Players sit in a circle. Every player except for one sits with eyes closed.

The other player walks around the outside of the circle and discreetly taps one player on the shoulder twice. That player is Onyx. The player to Onyx's right should be tapped on the shoulder once. That player is Onyx's helper.

Everyone now opens their eyes. The player who nominated Onyx can join in for fun (sitting anywhere other than between Onyx and Onyx's helper) or watch proceedings.

That same player begins by saying any single word or name in the English language.

Play passes to the left. The next player has 10 seconds to say a word or name that begins with the two, three or more letters at the end of the previous word or name.

Play continues in this way. A player who is unable to provide a word or name in the time available leaves the game.

For Onyx, the object of the game is to say the word 'Onyx'. Play then stops because there are no words which begin 'nyx-' or 'yx-' and Onyx is the winner.

For Onyx's helper, the idea is to feed Onyx a word which ends '-on' (or '-ony').

For everyone else, the object of the game is to keep play going until Onyx is eliminated when unable to think of a word in the 10 seconds (at which point they must declare that they were Onyx).

If only Onyx and Onyx's helper remain in the game, Onyx is the winner.

> **Variant**: *You can also play the game with no roles assigned. The object of the game is simply to be the first person to say 'Onyx'.*
>
> **Silly variant**: *Each player melds their word with the previous. So instead of 'traitor', 'torment', 'mental' . . . the turns would go 'traitor', 'traitorment', 'traitormental' . . . Players drop out if they mangle the melded word as it gets longer. The winner is the first to get to a melded word ending '-onyx', or the last to be eliminated, whichever comes first.*

• Turn to **182**.

'I have no idea who the Traitor is,' you say, 'but I'm absolutely sure that Amrit knew Isla was joking when she said she would murder him. I was there when she said it and he was laughing like a drain.'

Isla looks at you gratefully.

'I'm afraid that doesn't really change anything,' says Tim, sounding genuinely mournful. 'Amrit may well have believed it was a joke, but that has no bearing on whether it was actually true.' With that it's time to vote.

- Turn to **75**.

'Oh, I was just thinking about a duck I saw this morning,' you say.

'Fair enough!' say Precious.

The conversation moves on. The hive mind, if there is such a thing, alights on a topic that can't really be contentious: who has left the Castle (and won't be making a shock re-entry). It's funny to realise you haven't thought about, say, Steve-O or Elif for some time. You don't feel bad, though; you quite simply don't have the brain space.

- Turn to **192**.

51

You are invited out to the front steps of the Castle where your Host is waiting for you.

'So, you have banished a Traitor. You must all be feeling pretty happy with yourselves. But I have another surprise for you. Call it a reward. There will be no Conclave and therefore no murder tonight.' You all cheer spontaneously. 'But in exchange, after tomorrow's Mission, you will decide when the game ends. Either when there are three finalists left or you unanimously decide to end the game. But remember, if there is even a single Traitor amongst you, the Traitors will win.'

You head back inside where Ruby leads the celebrations, as she tops up people's drinks. But you are shaken. Tonight was too close for comfort. Gregg and Gabriel quiz you about how the Traitors tried to seduce you, what the wording on the card was. River sits and listens but seems shaken by the events at Round Table. You are relieved when the gong sounds and it is time for you to go up to your room.

You fall asleep turning over the various permutations in your head, and are, you think, relieved to wake to a pale sun. You have made it to the final day.

- Turn to **113**.

The more you think about it, the more you'd like some more information. Steve-O agrees with you, of course, as do Anna, Nina and Jorge. But the general mood seems a little impatient and the majority of people want to move to a vote. However, you make your stand and lead the way.

You ask some questions of Teddy about how his technique works, and you give Steve-O, who is clearly worked up, even more of a chance to incriminate himself.

'Faithfuls and Traitors,' announces your Host, 'it is time to carry out your first banishment. Please write down who you think should leave the game.'

When it comes to it, it's even tougher than you'd imagined. What if they're Faithfuls? It seems like Steve-O's a shoo-in for banishment, but you decide he deserves a fighting chance. And Irwin just doesn't add up as a Traitor in your mind. You vote for Tim.

But you were right to think that Steve-O was doomed. River and Laure go the same way as you, and Tim himself votes for Irwin. Other than that, it's time for Steve-O to leave. It's a big moment, watching him stand. His hands are shaking.

'Steve-O,' intones your Host. 'You have been banished. Before you leave the Castle, it's time to reveal whether you're Faithful or a Traitor.'

'I've gotta say,' offers Steve-O, 'I never thought I'd be going home this early. I had a lot of fight in me, I guess. Anyway.' He pauses. 'You messed up, guys. I'm a Faithful. Or was.'

'Oh Jesus!' barks Rakayah.

'This is on me, guys, I'm sorry, I rushed things,' offers Irwin. 'Steve-O, you're right, I'm so sorry, mate.' Teddy just stares ahead in silence.

YOU HAVE BANISHED A FAITHFUL.

- Turn to **244**.

53

You hear laughter from a nearby room and head along to the library.

'No,' says Teddy. 'Game theory is the key to all of this really.'

Irwin waves at you. 'Come and taxi over here for a bit, refuel.' You realise he's doing an airline pilot joke.

'Gregg (Salford, 29) has a very clever theory,' says Gabriel (Anglesey, 43). 'That they picked Luke because none of us will actually be able to work out why they picked him, which makes my head hurt to be honest, but I suppose that's why I wouldn't be a very good Traitor.' Something about the way Gabriel says it makes you look at him, though his gaze looks bright and open.

'Now, Teddy,' says Irwin. 'Explain this box chain to me again.'

'It's Blockchain,' says Teddy. 'Imagine that money is a . . .'

Taking that as your cue to leave, you get up quietly and slip out unnoticed. Time for some air.

- Turn to **105**.

54

As you trudge into the now familiar room, you feel sure it will feature in your dreams in the future. The dynamic has changed now there are fewer people. It feels more intimate and personal somehow. Everyone seems to know everyone's business in a way they couldn't when there were more people and they naturally broke up into smaller groups.

'Well, I'm happy to go first this time,' says Nina. But Gabriel leans forwards.

'I'm very sorry, Nina, but I have to ask you something first.' Nina looks shocked at the interruption but waves her hand in invitation.

'Nina, I really hate to ambush you, but I heard something quite shocking and I just need to be upfront with you. Someone has mentioned that Deb called you "Gran" earlier today. I have to ask. Are you related?'

Nina looks crestfallen. 'That's actually what I was about to say. Yes, Deb is my granddaughter.' There is a gasp in the room. 'I have wanted to tell you all so many times, but at first I didn't know people well enough, and then, well, winning would change Deb's life. And she deserves only good things. Living in different countries, I haven't always been able to be there for birthdays and Christmas. And she's such a good girl.' Her voice catches and she waves her hand in apology.

'I felt so guilty about being wrong about Isla. I thought you'd all hate me if you knew I was keeping this secret too.' Both Nina and Deb stare down at the table in shame.

There is silence for a moment, then Gregg says grumpily, 'Who told you, Gabriel?'

'Well, I'm not sure that's really—'

'I'd like to know too,' says Nina quietly.

'And I would like to know too,' says Jorge, frowning.

'It was me,' says River, but she's looking at you.

What do you do?

- Admit you heard it too. Turn to **39**.

- Keep quiet and hope River keeps the secret. Turn to **312**.

55

You mull over your choices as you brush your teeth. You think about what you could have done differently, but mostly you're glad you weren't one of the names getting voted for.

You replay the key moments from the day as you lay your head on the pillow. Will tonight be the night you're murdered?

You wake to birds singing and the sunlight streaming in through the gap in your curtains. You smell bacon cooking from below.

- Turn to **202**.

56

You vote for Ruby. Ruby votes for River. River votes for Ruby. Gabriel votes for Ruby. You did it! Your pact worked and you and River have both made it through.

'Ruby, you have been banished. Please tell us if you are Faithful or a Traitor.'

She steps forwards. 'I am so proud to have made it this far, even though I rejoined the game late. It's been a pleasure to get to know each and every one of you. But I'm afraid you made a mistake. I am a Faithful.' You don't even know if you need to but you still make sure you look shocked, shaking your head as Ruby is quietly led away.

'So,' says your Host. 'The final three. Please step forwards and reveal whether you are Faithful or a Traitor.'

Gabriel steps forwards, smiling. 'When I came in here, I knew I just wanted to be me, whatever else happened. I wanted to be true to myself. And that's why I'm so happy to say that I am a Faithful.'

River steps forwards and pauses. 'I've met people here that I'll never forget. It's been an unforgettable experience. But I'm sorry, Gabriel. I'm a Traitor.'

You step forwards solemnly, looking at Gabriel's distraught face. You don't have the heart to draw things out for dramatic effect. 'I'm sorry too, Gabriel. But I'm a Traitor as well.'

You and River exchange a look. Team Traitor did it!

YOU HAVE WON.

57

'I'm really only saying this to check in with everyone else, but I feel like I've noticed a bit of a change in Anna over the last couple of days. It seems as if she's been much less present with her odds and percentages. I don't know what that means; it's just something I've noticed.'

As soon as you've said it, you realise your error. Anna is utterly charming, as she explains that she no longer feels able to be so cold and abstract about people she now considers friends. Everyone nods along sympathetically.

Then Teddy looks at you sharply. 'I don't know about anyone else but it's not so much a change, more that you're always in the frame but somehow never get banished. And pretty much every time, we banish the wrong people. Maybe we need to stop making that mistake.'

You are shocked by the sharpness of his tone, and though you try to point out that you were actually the one who basically got rid of Rakayah, it sounds thin even to your ears. Gradually the room warms to Teddy's version of events and it's like dominoes falling as it is time for people to vote. You notice with a grim smile that even Precious and Ruby have been swayed by his argument.

It is no relief to see the shock in their eyes when you stand and tell them you're Faithful.

YOU HAVE BEEN BANISHED.

To play this day again, please turn to **295**. Better luck next time!

58

The mood is an odd mixture of celebration and mourning. Nina was so loved and the betrayal of her being a Traitor has hit everyone hard. People make an effort but it's clear their hearts aren't in it.

Only Anna seems her usual self and at one point even gives a long speech about how often people misjudge actual risk. 'People are scared of sharks, but only about eleven people a year die from shark attacks. Many more people are killed by vending machines falling on them. I guess Nina was our vending machine.'

As eulogies go, it's hard to beat.

The gong sounds and you head up to your room.

You are in bed, just reaching over to turn out your lamp when you hear a rustling sound under your bedroom door. You steel yourself for the worst – after all, who knows what might come under the door in this place. But when you look, it's an envelope. You jump down and open it up to read.

> *Faithful,*
>
> *You have been chosen to join the Traitors. Do you accept this offer, or refuse?*
>
> *Yours,*
>
> *The Traitors*

Your head is spinning. You have made it this far as a Faithful. Do you have what it takes to become a Traitor?

- Do you accept? Turn to **157**.

- Do you refuse? Turn to **273**.

59

You get ready for bed, brushing your teeth and looking at yourself in the mirror. You again think how often things come down to the right line of argument in the Round Table. Perhaps it would be possible to avoid that if you get to know people a little better.

You sleep fitfully, your dreams full of shadowy figures who mean you harm. But you wake to a bright dawn. You have survived another day.

- Turn to **130**.

BONUS GAME

CAPTURE THE CASTLE: SWINDLER

You need: deck of cards, phone with timer

Players: Town Crier, plus at least two others

Take from the deck two 2s (the Renegades) and one 3 (the Swindler). Then add court cards (king, queen, jack) until there are three more cards than there are players.

One player is the Town Crier and should now read the text below.

I am shuffling the cards, and dealing one to everyone, including myself.

I am now placing the remaining cards face down in a row on the table.

Everyone, look at your card. If you have a 2, you are a Renegade, come to capture the castle. If you have a 3, you are the Swindler. Everyone else is a member of the Royal Family.

Place your card face down, close to the three already on the table in a way that makes it clear whose is whose.

When I say 'Let us dance!', the Masked Ball will commence. Everyone – including me – will close their eyes for a count of eight. During that time, any Renegades must open their eyes and clock each other.

Ready . . . Let us dance! One, two, three, four, five, six, seven . . . eight.

Everyone must open their eyes. The King has heard that there may be a Renegade at his Masked Ball. In five minutes' time, he will have someone put in the stocks. You have five minutes to debate whom to place in the stocks. Any of you may claim to have been assigned any of the identities: Royal Family, Renegade or Swindler, whether this is true or false. But the Swindler may only tell lies.

The time starts . . . now.

Set the timer, and then when the time is up . . .

After a count of five, we shall all vote. The player or players with the most votes shall be placed in the stocks.

If one or more Renegades is placed in the stocks, the Royal Family shall be declared victorious. If there were no Renegades, the Royal Family shall be declared victorious. In all other situations, the Renegades shall be declared victorious. If you decide that the King should exhibit clemency, you should now agree to each vote for the player on your left, and nobody shall be put in the stocks.

I shall now make the count of five. One, two, three, four, five.

NB: this game can be combined with other Capture the Castle games in the list of games at the start of the book, so long as the total number of cards is always topped up to three more than the number of players using members of the Royal Family.

After the game, you decide to go for a stroll with Alexis.

- Turn to **136**.

61

'It's just a hunch . . .' opens Gregg. You try to look as collected as possible, and at the same time to avoid looking like you're trying to look collected – and you realise that Gregg is taking things in a direction that's completely different to the one you feared. He says that he's not the best person to open the discussion (how modest, you ruefully observe) and says he'd like to 'pass the conch shell' to Anna.

You can't decide if Gregg is being sadistic and drawing out the tension for you, or whether you have invented the whole thing in your own head. You think back to this morning. Was it possible that Gregg hadn't been mounting a whisper campaign against you?

- Turn to **205**.

62

'Now,' says your Host. 'This is where things get really serious. If you are absolutely confident that all of you are Faithfuls, then we can stop the game now. But remember, if there is a Traitor here, then they have won. So, if you wish, you can make the decision to banish one further person. Which will you choose?' Your Host gestures for you to look next to you. 'Beside you is a chest with two ceremonial pouches in it. One is labelled "End Game". The other "Banish Again". When you have made your decision, hand over your chosen pouch and we will reveal your decision. If any one of you chooses to banish again, you all must.'

Your head is spinning. In the whirl of elation at making it through to this stage, you hadn't even thought that this might not be the end. But of course there is one final twist. You look around you. Ruby is frowning and looking at River. Gabriel looks serene.

Aware that every move will be scrutinised, you confidently grab the 'End Game' pouch and hand it over, trying with every sinew of your being to communicate breezy confidence in your fellow Faithfuls. If there's even the chance of ending the game now, you have to take it, whatever you might have just said.

'First, Gabriel,' says your Host. Another pouch and green smoke, curling up into the night sky, lit by the flames. *End Game.*

When your pouch goes into the fire, the smoke is green, swirling around you. *End Game.*

'Now, Ruby,' says your Host. Appropriately, the smoke is lit ruby. *Banish Again.*

'Now, River,' says your Host. The pouch is thrown into the fire and red smoke rises. *Banish Again.*

'So,' your Host says, 'you're not sure. Time to take your slates and write the name of who you will now, finally, banish.'

What do you do?

- Write Gabriel. Turn to **193**.

- Write River. Turn to **91**.

- Write Ruby. Turn to **88**.

63

You are invited out to the front steps of the Castle where your Host is waiting for you.

'So, you have banished a Traitor. You must all be feeling pretty happy with yourselves. But I have another surprise for you. Call it a reward. There will be no Conclave and therefore no murder tonight.' You all cheer spontaneously. 'But in exchange, after tomorrow's Mission, you will decide when the game ends. When you are absolutely confident there are no remaining Traitors, simply tell me and we will end the game. But remember, if there is even a single Traitor amongst you, the Traitors will win.'

Back inside, Ruby leads the celebrations, as she tops up people's drinks. But you are shaken. Tonight was too close for comfort. You make sure to join in with the disbelief that Tim was a Traitor. You feel terrible about turning on him. But it was the only way.

You never thought you'd miss the chance to meet River and discuss the night in the Conclave, but you really do!

Though you should fall asleep easily, you sleep fitfully with dreams full of betrayal and recrimination, and wake to a pale sun. You have made it to the final day.

- Turn to **267**.

64

'Ruby is too obvious,' you say. 'But we could do the next best thing and break her up from her closest confidante.' River nods enthusiastically.

'You're right, we can't go for Ruby,' says Tim. 'Not after she came for me so hard earlier. It'll look like straight revenge and put a target on my back. But I do love the idea of breaking up Precious and Ruby. They're becoming a right little unit. Is it too obvious that we're doing that to get to Ruby though?'

You have an idea. 'Could we try and spin that it was exactly what a ruthless Traitor would do?' Both of them nod along. You all decide to murder Precious.

- Turn to **18**.

65

DAY 11

You arrive downstairs first. Breakfast is the quietest it's ever been, which is useful because your mind is racing. Last night was intense and you couldn't sleep, as you were agonising over whether you should have told the others about the Traitors' attempt to seduce you. On the one hand, why give away something like this for free, when you could use it more strategically if you need to . . . but is there a point at which it feels you've been holding the information back too long? You feel your insides churning with emotion.

One by one, the knock at the door and then the wave and the smile: Gregg, Gabriel, River and finally Tim, making a shocked face as he comes around the door. And then it's just Ruby and Precious left. There is a babble of nervous conversation. Everyone looks around the room and realises: Precious hasn't made it.

You see Ruby quietly wiping at her eyes. River goes and sits with her, squeezing her arm. The fact she is still here is interesting. She had gone hard after Anna and Tim. So if Tim was a Traitor, he might have tried to get rid of her, but that would have looked too obvious. Unless Ruby is playing an incredible double bluff and got rid of the last person anyone would have suspected her to get rid of. Then again, all the Traitors would have seen Ruby leading the charge and might be triple-bluffing by making it look like she got rid of her best friend. Your brain hurts.

Gregg's gone very quiet. You think back to last night's flicker of something passing between Tim and him. Is that because they are a unit like Anna said? He always seems to take these things hard.

Tim and Gabriel are still sitting together, in a group with you.

River pipes up. 'Cheer up everyone! We might not have got rid of a Traitor. But we're one day closer to the end. We're nearly there, guys.' Everyone nods and smiles at her.

It feels as if everyone is a suspect now.

As you're all leaving, you think you see a gesture from Ruby. If you had to translate it into words, it would be something like 'Would you hang back?'

What do you do?

- Wait for Ruby. Turn to **97**.

- Leave with everyone else. Turn to **87**.

66

In the hall, people are milling about. Apparently people are being called in one by one to meet with the Host. Sitting in a large wooden chair in the hall is Anna (Whitley Bay, 72), who after smiling hello tells you she's an actuary, then leaves a pause for you to respond. 'Is that like an accountant?' you offer. The answer is yes and no, apparently. 'It's about understanding risk. Everyone always thinks it's about numbers, but it's actually about people, so you can see why I think I'll be good in here.' You don't exactly see, and ask her name again. 'Sorry,' you say, 'so many new names.' Just then, Jorge (Folkestone, 60) walks by. 'Now he's a dentist,' she says. 'I could tell you some stories around the risk connected to dentistry. I'm glad he's got a nice smile, though. Never trust a dentist with bad teeth.'

You are joined by Luke, who walks over arm in arm with Nina. 'I seem to have picked up this fancy man in the drawing room,' she twinkles. 'I am terrible with names,' says Luke in response. 'Proper rubbish, actually. Which is weird because I'm a quantity surveyor.' You nod and smile but have absolutely no idea how those things are connected.

- Turn to **12**.

One by one, everyone heads off, until it's just you and River.

'It's nice to have Gregg back with us, isn't it?' she says. 'Feels like he went a bit AWOL there for a while, what with Nina and Flowergate and then Tim.' She is fanning herself with a straw hat.

'I've been mentioning that to people,' she follows up quickly. 'I thought you might like to consider that too?' So she's appealing to Team Traitor. After the ease with which she disposed of Tim last night, you're not sure you trust her at all.

You look around you, to check if anyone is nearby.

What do you do?

- Agree with River. Turn to **37**.

- Keep things vague. Turn to **16**.

Tim stands over by the window and watches Gregg walking across the lawn in the distance. 'Well, there's a Traitor-hunter with the weight of the world on his shoulders,' he says. 'I should really go and talk to him.'

'I'm not sure if looking sad because you've banished a Traitor would be my strategy,' says Anna. 'If I was advising his life insurer, I'd say there was some extra risk there!'

You realise that might be the first time you've heard Anna make a joke.

'The way I see it, Gregg's behaviour makes sense as one of two options,' says Anna. 'Either he is genuinely shocked by the news that Nina was a Traitor. Or he's a Traitor who threw Nina under the bus and feels guilty.'

You nod along. It's certainly an interesting choice of behaviour from Gregg. And one which could be useful to you and the other Traitors.

'I would never argue with you on strategy, Anna,' says Tim, 'but I have a question. Do you feel as confident making predictions about the people who just keep themselves to themselves?'

'Like who?'

He pauses. 'Like Ruby, say? Or Precious?' As ever with Tim, it's said with a very breezy tone, but there's something a little forceful about it. 'Or perhaps it's just that I've never liked "Ruby Tuesday" as a song.' He has his eyes closed but you see the others looking at him, a little bemused. You can see what he's doing, trying to keep Gregg in the game, because he sees him as less of a threat than Ruby. But he has to be careful he isn't too out of step with everyone else. At this stage, overconfidence could be fatal.

'Well, there's certainly less data to go on,' concedes Anna. 'If she is a Traitor, then her question about whether anyone has changed their behaviour was very clever. Because it made her seem like she was rooting out Traitors, but, of course, we don't know her, so can't judge if *her* behaviour has changed. Precious is even more of a mystery as she's taken much more of a back seat. It's just the sort of devious thing to happen in this place for them to send in a Traitor.'

Tim sips from his tea, looking thoughtful. You chat for a while and then decide it's time for a change of scene. You are suddenly aware of making sure your behaviour stays the same.

- Turn to **46**.

69

'I don't believe it, I just don't believe it,' says Elif.

You sit in shock between Tim and Teddy in the bar, as people mutter among themselves.

'I was so sure,' says Teddy.

'Don't be too harsh on yourself, lad,' says Tim, patting his hand. 'Anyone can make a mistake.'

As you sit, you realise how quickly people can turn at Round Table. The evening is a blur of names and faces, as you try to learn more about the people you're meeting. You talk to Anna about your maths teachers when you were growing up, and sit with Gregg and Deb as they discuss where they like to go out at home. At one point, Rakayah makes Jorge sing a song to Isla and Amrit, and everyone has to admit he's surprisingly good.

The gong signals that it's time for bed.

- Turn to **55**.

It feels good to be getting to know people from scratch again. Precious is doing a master's in media and communication, which she is sure will be useful in the Castle.

Ruby is a genome researcher, but when Gabriel asks what that is, her explanation only makes everyone more confused.

'Crumbs,' laughs Tim. 'That almost made me ask Teddy about what Bigcoins are again.'

'It's Bitcoins,' says Teddy.

'I did say nearly ask you,' says Tim. Everyone laughs and the conversation moves on. As the sun tracks across the room, everyone wishes they could postpone this moment before Round Table. But soon enough it is time to go in.

'Mainly, I can't stop thinking about what it must be like to be a Traitor right now,' says Precious as she stands up. 'You've probably got used to it, but it feels so strange that literally in this room are people who are lying about who they are.'

- Turn to **177**.

Now that you know the Traitors are among you, you're told that it's time to relax. The irony of this is lost on no one. You're not sure how to relax, or what to do, if you're honest with yourself, so you're quite relieved to hear that you're all going to be told what the rest of the evening holds.

Then your Host appears looking down on you all from the staircase.

'Well, well. Welcome, Traitors. You may be working against the Faithfuls, but you will also have to work together every day to complete Missions. And now it's time for your first one. Good luck!'

People are smiling nervously as you all gather together, no one sure what to expect.

- Turn to **24**.

You all make your way outside to where your Host is waiting.

'Greetings, Faithfuls and Traitors, it is time for you to stop your battle and work together for the good of the Mission.'

MISSION

MONEY IN THE BANK

You need: coins (about five per player) and a bag, pencil and paper

Players: four or more

Begin by writing the words 'Bank Robber' on two pieces of paper (if the players number four, five or six); on three pieces of paper (if the players number seven or eight); or four pieces of paper (if you number nine or more). Write 'Bank Clerk' on enough pieces of paper so that there's one for each player.

Mix up the pieces of paper and distribute them randomly.

When you all know your role, everyone closes their eyes.

On a count of three, only the Bank Robbers open their eyes, and see who is who.

The oldest player suggests a team of any size (which may include his or herself) to go in to the bank. All players vote on whether they approve of the team. If there is not a majority approval, the oldest player suggests another team.

Once a team is chosen, each of its members takes a coin and decides whether to place it with heads or tails showing. Everyone closes their eyes while the team's members place their coins on the table.

If there are mostly heads, the coins are safe and go in the bag. Otherwise, the coins are removed from play: they have been stolen.

Next, the player to the left of the oldest player suggests a team and the action repeats. The Bank Robbers aim to steal as much money as possible. The Bank Clerks aim to identify the thieves and minimise the bank's losses.

Play stops when all coins are either in the bag or stolen.

NB: all coins have the same value for the purposes of Money in the Bank.

As you're leaving the Mission, Deb, Gregg and Jorge say they want to pick your brain about a theory Alexis had mentioned that the two of you had discussed, and would you join them in the library?

You are slightly startled, though of course on some level you assume everyone is talking about everyone else. Do you really want to have theories attached to you though?

What do you do?

- Go with them to the library. Turn to **298**.

- Make polite excuses and head off in the other direction. Turn to **9**.

73

One by one, everyone heads off, until it's just you and River.

'It's nice to have Gregg back with us, isn't it?' she says. 'Feels like he went a bit AWOL there for a while, what with Nina and then Tim.' She is fanning herself with a straw hat.

'Which totally makes sense,' she follows up quickly. 'I don't think there's anything untoward there, do you?'

When you look up, she's watching you intently. It feels as if she's fishing, but should you respond to the bait?

What do you do?

- Engage with River. Turn to **140**.

- Just shrug and keep things vague. Turn to **213**.

74

It's a welcome break, getting a bit of peace and quiet in your room.

But there's no breakthrough moment.

You contemplate how you don't know what the Traitors were up to last night, you don't know how many of them there are, and you'd be very hard pressed to say who they are.

On the other hand, last night's banishment finally went the way that it's supposed to. So perhaps things are turning?

Resolved to keep thinking positive thoughts, you head back downstairs.

- Turn to **294**.

75

As everyone holds up their slates, it becomes clear that, a couple of votes for Deb aside, Isla is gone.

Even you have written her name down, reasoning that if she is a goner, it makes sense to join in with the masses, rather than having to come up with another name and risk annoying or threatening anyone else.

She stands in front of everyone, smiling bitterly.

'Congratulations all of you. With your brilliant reading of people . . .' Deb leans forwards in delight.

'You just banished another Faithful.'

There is an audible groan.

YOU HAVE BANISHED A FAITHFUL.

- Turn to **237**.

76

After the Mission, where for the first time you were part of the winning team, you, Ruby and Gregg head to the Armoury. You walk down a long corridor to a cool, dark room full of suits of armour and glass cabinets containing long, sharp things. You enter the private chamber and are faced with the numbered chests. For no particular reason, you pick chest three, only to find it empty. Once, this would have meant so much more, but now it merits only a shrug. As you all head back up from the Armoury, you hang back a bit so it's just you and Gregg.

'Weird one last night?' you say.

He nods. 'It's weird because I should be really happy. But I never thought Nina was a Traitor, I was just genuinely confused by the florist thing. And now I feel like I don't know anything. I'm half hoping I get banished tonight, to be honest. I'm not sure I've got it in me any more.' He seems so down that you have to say something.

'Oh, don't say that,' you say. 'It's all part of the game, isn't it?'

'I know, and that's what Tim has been saying to me, trying to make me feel better. I just know that everyone is off gossiping about me and I feel like I have this massive target on my back.' You can't help but feel that Gregg could be an extremely useful distraction at Round Table, the less he knows. But equally he's not a complete fool.

What do you do?

- Be honest and say that people were a little taken aback by the way he's been behaving. Turn to **23**.

- Try not to stress him out and say there's not a problem. Turn to **114**.

77

'OK,' he says, 'I genuinely am saying this because I don't know what to think. But Nina and I went off on a long walk in the gardens and it was all great and then she mentioned something about someone in her office at work. And I think, office, that's weird. I don't know much about floristry but I don't reckon it's very office-based, so I asked her if that was the back office of the florist shop and she caught herself and was a bit weird. And then she told me that she was actually only a florist for a couple of years and that for most of her career she worked in investment banking. She quit because she stopped believing in what she was doing but that she was basically a really senior banker. Isn't that a bit messed up?'

You meet his gaze. 'I don't want to be confrontational, but it doesn't sound a million miles away from crime-novelist-gate to me.'

'Oh come on, I think accidentally not specifying which bit of the media you work in is a bit different to an entirely different type of job! I'm not saying it makes her a Traitor, I just can't get my head around why she'd lie.'

'Maybe,' you say, 'and I'm spitballing here, but maybe she just wanted people to get to know her and not hear about her job and make assumptions. It hasn't been a brilliant decade for bankers. It certainly feels like something that she should be allowed to respond to.'

'So you think I should raise it before Round Table?' he asks.

'If I was you, that's what I'd do,' you say.

'Thank you,' he says, and heads downstairs.

- Turn to **118**.

78

The atmosphere that night is low. Ruby and Precious sit on their own. Tim is quiet with his own thoughts. Gregg looks on the verge of tears.

River is pretty subdued, as is Gabriel, and you suppose you must come across like that too. Inside, all you can think is that you can't wait to go to the Conclave and talk about tonight.

Later that night you lie on the bed waiting until it's time to tiptoe up to the Conclave.

- Turn to **260**.

You dive in and say that you actually feel quite sorry for Laure, and that you liked her. You pause while you think of what to say next. You add that you were always convinced that she was Faithful, and that this proves it.

That all seems a bit vague, so you add that you'll miss her. And you decide to deal directly with the incident Gregg is referring to: you say that the pair of you were discussing breakfasts yesterday and the chat probably went on a bit too long. 'For both of us.'

You can hear in yourself that you're starting to ramble a bit. You pause.

Gregg and a few others are discussing how tonight there's absolutely no way that you can all banish another Faithful. Rakayah is agreeing loudly.

You agree too but, as you walk away, you feel you could have done a better job when you were talking about Laure.

- Turn to **6**.

80

'I've spoken a lot to Alexis today and I don't think she's a Traitor. I made the decision when I came in here that I would be entirely myself. One hundred per cent honest. That's who I am. And you've all asked me questions and I've told you what I honestly think. I haven't been guiding anything. I've just been honest. To me that's the mark of a Faithful. But can everyone around the table say the same?' You look at David, almost enjoying the melodrama of it. 'Dave, is there anything you'd like to share with the group?'

He looks down at the table, shamefaced. Then it all comes spilling out. How he's lied. How there is no pub and how sorry he is.

Deb and Rakayah look heartbroken. Deb says, 'The one thing I can't stand in life is a liar.' You don't need to do any more. The conversation leads inexorably to the inevitable question – if he was lying about that, what else might he be lying about? When it's time to write a name, almost everyone, you included, writes down David's name.

He stands in front of everyone.

'Well, David,' says the Host. 'You have been chosen to leave. But are you Faithful or a Traitor?'

'I just want to say again to everyone how sorry I am that I lied. But I'm a Faithful.'

There is an audible gasp and Deb shouts out, 'Nooooooo!'

- Turn to **241**.

81

As if to undermine the seriousness of what is to come, it's a beautiful morning and you catch up with River and Ruby as they're heading down the steps towards one of the walled gardens.

'We thought we'd better make the most of it, as any one of us could be leaving in the next few hours,' says River.

You walk along a gravel path and through into a redbrick garden with neat rows of vegetables and herbs. Bees fly lazily in between plants.

'Well, come on then,' says River to Ruby. 'You always have a working theory.'

'I've got nothing,' says Ruby. 'My plan has been to watch everyone's reaction really carefully at the last couple of banishments, to see if there was anything unusual that was a clue. But they're such emotional events, it's really hard to know what the normal way to react is.'

'That's so true,' says River. 'It's like at school when the teacher would say whoever did the thing needs to own up, and even though you know you didn't do it, you feel like you're acting guiltily. I one hundred per cent know I'm a Faithful, but I'm still there second-guessing my reactions.'

You nod along. 'I feel like we constantly find a frame that explains behaviour as odd or suspicious,' you say. 'But it's actually just that this is a fundamentally odd situation.'

As you walk past strawberry plants under a net, you try and think back to the last couple of banishments. What clues might there have been?

As you reach the other side of the garden, you explain you're going to head back inside and they wave you away.

- Turn to **300**.

82

With N people, it's four times N, plus one. If you got it right, let's hope your sound judgement also means you'll escape banishment and murder. If you didn't get it right . . . well, good luck.

- Turn to **38**.

83

You manage it. And you manage to think of something to say, which is a relief. It's not the most profound speech – essentially you reiterate how important it is that the group stops losing Faithfuls – but you start to feel a little more confident than you have for most of the day.

As soon as you finish, though, Gregg clears his throat again. The risk of talking over him twice seems too great, so you just try to look as calm – and innocent – as possible. What do innocent people look like, though, you worry? And don't people who are actively trying to look innocent – whether they're guilty or not – look guilty as hell?

You can't decide if Gregg is being sadistic and drawing out the tension for you, or whether you have invented the whole thing in your own head. You think back to this morning. Was it possible that Gregg hadn't been mounting a whisper campaign against you?

As you perform this painful mental yoga, it dawns on you that Gregg isn't talking about Laure. And he isn't talking about you. He is – kind of imperiously, you think – giving his judgement on who is the best person to open the discussion. And it's Anna.

- Turn to **205**.

After breakfast, a group of you continue your tradition of finishing your teas and coffees over a game in the library.

BONUS GAME

CAPTURE THE CASTLE: CLAIRVOYANT

You need: deck of cards, phone with timer

Players: Town Crier, plus at least two others

Take from the deck two 2s (the Renegades) and one 5 (the Clairvoyant). Then add court cards (king, queen, jack) until there are three more cards than there are players.

One player is the Town Crier and should now read the text below.

I am shuffling the cards, and dealing one to everyone, including myself.

I am now placing the remaining cards face down in a row on the table.

Everyone, look at your card. If you have a 2, you are a Renegade, come to capture the castle. If you have a 5, you are the Clairvoyant. Everyone else is a member of the Royal Family. Place your card face down, close to the three already on the table in a way that makes it clear whose is whose.

When I say, 'Let us dance!', the Masked Ball will commence. Everyone – including me – will close their eyes for a count of eight. During that time, any Renegades must open their eyes and clock each other.

Ready . . . Let us dance! One, two, three, four, five, six, seven . . . eight.

Everyone must open their eyes. When I say, 'Send for the Clairvoyant!', we will all again close our eyes for a count of eight. During that time, the Clairvoyant may silently look at one other player's card.

Ready . . . Send for the Clairvoyant! One, two, three, four, five, six, seven . . . eight.

Everyone must open their eyes. The King has heard that there may be a Renegade at his Masked Ball. In five minutes' time, he will have someone placed in the stocks. You have five minutes to debate whom to place in the stocks. Any of you may claim to have been assigned any of the identities: Royal Family, Renegade or Clairvoyant.

The time starts . . . now.

Set the timer, and then when the time is up . . .

After a count of five, we shall all vote. The player or players with the most votes shall be placed in the stocks.

If one or more Renegades is placed in the stocks, the Royal Family shall be declared victorious. If there were no Renegades, the Royal Family shall be declared victorious. In all other situations, the Renegades shall be declared victorious. If you decide that the King should exhibit clemency, you should now agree to each vote for the player on your left, and nobody shall be placed in the stocks.

I shall now make the count of five. One, two, three, four, five.

NB: this game can be combined with other Capture the Castle games in the list of games at the start of the book, so long as the total number of cards is always topped up to three more than the number of players using members of the Royal Family.

• Turn to **188**.

You chip in, admitting that you have heard Tim's name a few times from various people, but that to be honest, you've heard Anna's name mentioned just as often too. After that speech last night, when she seemed like the only one who was happy and relieved, and now today hearing Tim, you just think there's something not quite right.

You do a quick totting-up in your head and work out that Tim has almost certainly got the votes over Anna. He's made it a straight popularity contest and he's almost certainly going to win. At this stage, voting with the Traitors but not standing out is the perfect result for you.

As the names are revealed, Anna, Ruby and Precious all vote for Tim, restating their original reasoning, but the rest of you vote for Anna. River goes first and says, 'I just didn't hear that passion when you were defending yourself that I'd expect if you were a Faithful.' Everyone else gives some version of that too.

Your Host steps forwards. 'Let's see if you've got it right. Anna, please tell the room, are you Faithful or a Traitor?'

She stands in front of you with a calm smile on her face.

'The numbers never lie. I am a Faithful.'

There is a collective groan. 'I told you,' says Ruby in disgust.

YOU HAVE BANISHED A FAITHFUL.

- Turn to **78**.

86

'I'll go first this time,' you say. 'And it was actually something you said earlier, Ruby, that made me think of this.' She has a look of apprehension on her face. 'You said that it was hard to know what normal behaviour was in this environment. And that got me thinking that you've had an advantage coming in late, as we haven't got to know you yet. You've led the charge a couple of times against people who've turned out to be Traitors. But who knows if you just want to win on your own? I look at you and I see a very intelligent, capable young woman. A perfect Traitor.'

Ruby is shocked for a moment, before she goes on the offensive. She points out how illogical it would be for her to enter the Castle as a Traitor and then proceed to wipe out her fellow Traitors. She points out that everyone has got to know her a bit by now and knows she's logical and pragmatic.

She seems genuinely disappointed that you've turned on her like this and concludes that the only reason for it must be that you are desperately trying to distract people from your own increasingly erratic behaviour. She says that this behaviour has made up her mind. You are a Traitor.

Gabriel says he's surprised by your accusation as this wasn't what you were saying earlier. River agrees that this feels like it bears little relationship to conversations you had earlier. Gregg can clearly see which way the wind is blowing and says something vague about seeing everyone's point of view.

When the names are written, you vote for Ruby, but everyone else votes for you. To come so close but so far from winning burns. You can't help but feel you played your cards poorly.

'I am . . . a Traitor,' you say. No one remembers the name of the horse that falls at the final fence. You could kick yourself.

YOU HAVE BEEN BANISHED.

To play this day again, please turn to **267**. Better luck next time!

You head out with everyone else, your head still spinning after last night's events.

You end up sitting with River and Tim as she tries to explain horoscopes to Tim.

'I've just never understood how everyone could possibly be one of twelve things,' says Tim. 'And it's always "Geminis are very friendly but can be unfriendly if wronged, so they have their cake and eat it."' River is fanning herself with a straw hat, smiling.

'I sometimes doubt we really even need twelve,' says River, laughing. 'I think I could put all my exes into one group.' You chat for a bit longer, but you're happy to take a back seat and listen to them, chipping in only when absolutely necessary.

Both of them say they're too hot and head inside but you stay outside, grateful for the private moment. A couple of minutes later, Gabriel comes and sits next to you. For a moment you toy with telling him about your secret. It would feel so good to tell someone and have one person you are being completely honest with. But you decide against it.

'Want to hear Ruby's latest theories?' he asks. You nod and he leans in. 'So, you, me and Gregg seem to have somehow snuck through because of stupidity, niceness and just general trustworthiness. But she's on the fence about River and actively going for Tim. What do you think?'

What do you do?

- Agree she might be onto something with River. Turn to **143**.

- Say that Tim is where your suspicions lie. Turn to **104**.

Reasoning that River will vote for her too, you write Ruby. Ruby writes River. River has written your name. (So much for loyalty!) Gabriel has written your name. Your Host addresses you as you step forwards. 'So, you have been banished, but are you Faithful or a Traitor?'

You step forwards. 'I'm so happy to have made it to the end. I've learnt so much here. That's why it was so hard to lie to you. But I am a Traitor.'

There is a mood of celebration and Gabriel and Ruby can't help but smile.

YOU HAVE BEEN BANISHED.

To play this day again, please turn to **267**. Better luck next time!

As you're walking across the landing from your room, you approach a large ornamental vase on a plinth. It looks like there's someone behind it. You think to yourself: are they hiding? Then you tell yourself to stop reading too much into things.

But there is someone there. Gregg. He's gazing out of the window, apparently deep in thought. He looks up as you approach.

'You seem like you're miles away,' you say.

'Oh, I'm just feeling a bit under the spotlight at the moment. I feel like whatever I do is really suspect and I'm slightly dreading Round Table tonight.'

You try to keep your face neutral but he nods. 'So they're actively considering me, are they?

'Listen, I heard something from Nina earlier, and I really don't know what to think. Can I talk to you about it?'

Every time you've encountered secrets, things have got tricky. It may turn out to be gossip, but can you turn down the chance to get some new information?

What do you do?

- Tell Gregg that if he's learnt something he should share it with the whole group. Turn to **33**.

- Listen to what Gregg has to say. Turn to **77**.

'I just think we really need to be thinking about people's motives more deeply.' The three of them nod along. 'I've noticed there's a tendency to treat the Traitors as if they're going to be thinking very simply. But they're among us. They're having exactly the same conversations as we all are.'

'One of us could be a Traitor,' says Deb. 'I mean, I'm not. I couldn't be. But other people are.'

For a while you compare notes on who has been spending time with each other and who hasn't (making sure not to mention the people in the room with you).

As you leave, you bump into Nina and Rakayah walking down the corridor arm in arm. 'I hope I'm as active as you when I'm your age,' says Rakayah. 'I just think you're *marvellous.*'

You nod at them and follow them down the corridor to where Teddy is standing, who says, 'It's Round Table time.'

- Turn to **141**.

Reasoning that you really can't trust her, you decide that attack is the best form of defence and you write River. Ruby writes River. River has written your name. You're clearly both as loyal as each other. Gabriel has written your name.

'Now there is a tiebreak,' says your Host. 'You will each get two minutes to convince your fellow Contestants to break the deadlock.'

You have one final choice to try and win. But what should you do? Who should you target to change their mind, Gabriel or River? Should you try and form an alliance with River to make sure the Traitors win? Or do you go for broke and try and win the game solo by getting rid of her?

What do you do?

- Convince Gabriel to vote for River. Turn to **22**.

- Convince River to vote for Gabriel. Turn to **15**.

92

Yes! With three people, it's 13. You have one final (harder) question to answer. Return to **96** and continue.

93

You just can't bring yourself to be honest with him when he's so down.

'I wouldn't worry about it,' you say. 'We're all a bit bruised by last night. I think most people, if they think anything about it, just think that you're sensitive.'

'What, even Ruby?' he says.

You're unable to hide the look on your face.

'Thank you,' he says. 'I really appreciate you trying to make me feel better. It's a very kind thing to do.'

Up ahead, Gabriel calls back, 'Everyone's going to play a game in the library!' You both quicken your pace to catch up with the others.

- Turn to **240**.

94

'Now,' says your Host. 'This is where things get really serious. If you are absolutely confident that all of you are Faithfuls, then we can stop the game now. But remember, if there is a Traitor here, then they have won. So, if you wish, you can make the decision to banish one further person. Which will you choose?' Your Host gestures for you to look next to you. 'Beside you is a chest with two ceremonial pouches in it. One is labelled "End Game". The other "Banish Again". When you have made your decision, hand over your chosen pouch and we will reveal your decision.'

Your head is spinning. In the whirl of elation at making it through to this stage, you hadn't even thought that this might not be the end. But of course there is one final twist. You look around you. Ruby is frowning and looking at River. Gabriel looks serene.

Aware that every move will be scrutinised, you confidently grab the 'End Game' pouch and hand it over, trying with every sinew of your being to communicate breezy confidence in your fellow Faithfuls. If there's even the chance of ending the game now, you have to take it, whatever you might have just said.

'First, Gabriel,' says your Host. Another pouch and green smoke, curling up into the night sky, lit by the flames. *End Game*.

When your pouch goes into the fire, the smoke is green, swirling around you. *End Game*.

'Now, Ruby,' says your Host. Appropriately, the smoke is lit ruby. *Banish Again*.

'Now, River,' says your Host. The pouch is thrown into the fire and red smoke rises. *Banish Again*.

'So,' your Host says, 'you're not sure. Time to take your slates and write the name of who you will now banish.' You try and read from River's expression whether or not she's going to try and win as the only Traitor at this final moment, or whether she'll be loyal to the end.

What do you do?

- Write Gabriel. Turn to **262**.

- Write River. Turn to **231**.

- Write Ruby. Turn to **56**.

95

Everyone is sitting together in the library and for the first time in what feels like ages, the mood is happy.

'It's so weird to be here,' says Precious.

Ruby nods along vigorously. 'So weird. We need to know every-thing!' Everyone starts talking at once.

It's fascinating to see how hungry everyone is for new company. And you note how Precious and Ruby have naturally become a unit. You can't decide if it's ultimately an advantage or not to come in late like this. On one hand, they don't have much time to build relationships and form alliances. On the other hand, they haven't had to survive. And perhaps no one will feel able to banish them so soon. You'd certainly think twice about it. It would feel cruel.

'You're very quiet,' says Ruby, looking at you.

What do you do?

- Come clean about what you were thinking. Turn to **247**.

- Make up something vague to cover yourself. Turn to **50**.

MISSION

ROWBOAT

At the end of your walk is a little jetty. There's another on the other side of the river. There's a rowboat moored at the jetty, as you might expect. And there is a collection of empty suits of armour shining in the midday sun, which you definitely didn't expect.

Rakayah and Jorge are instructed to wear the armour. Getting it on takes a while, even with the help of the valets. Once they're sweltering inside, you're told the nature of the task.

You and Ruby (still both in twenty-first-century clothing) are teamed with Rakayah and Jorge. You must all get to the other side of the river. But the boat can only withstand two (normal) adults. And someone in a suit of armour weighs twice as much as they normally would.

Is it possible, and if so, what is the minimum number of trips needed? Take a moment and see if you can work it out.

What do you think?

- *I think it's impossible.* Turn to **107**.

- *I think it's 9.* Turn to **179**.

- *I think it's 11.* Turn to **199**.

You're now joined by Gabriel, who, as you might by now have guessed, is clad in armour. He's another one who weighs twice as much. How many trips is it going to take now?

- *I think it's 10.* Turn to **40**.

- *I think it's 12.* Turn to **162**.

- *I think it's 13.* Turn to **92**.

And your final question: what if you and Ruby were joined by a given number of your associates (represented by *N*), all wearing armour? Can you work out the formula for how many trips *that* would take?

- Commit your answer to memory and turn to **82**.

- When you are finished, turn to **38**.

97

Ruby makes to leave but then reverses as if she's forgotten something. 'I wanted to ask you privately, as I feel like you'll give me a straightforward answer.'

'Thanks,' you say. 'I think.' For a moment you wonder if she somehow knows your secret about the seduction. But how?

'Do you think they got rid of Precious to get to me?' Phew.

'What do you mean?'

'The Traitors. I went after Tim and even though he was able to turn the room, he's still my number one suspect. The way I see it, Gregg is too dim to have it in him. Gabriel is either a genius socio-pathic Traitor, or just actually is that nice. River couldn't give out more Faithful vibes if she was wearing a white cloak, which actu-ally makes me think I need to watch her a bit more. I feel like you're definitely a Faithful. So that leaves Tim as my only definite. We have to pay close attention to everything Tim and River do.'

You think carefully about how to respond.

What do you do?

- Agree that Tim is in your thoughts too. Turn to **195**.

- Say that actually River feels like a better bet. Turn to **13**.

98

This is not the case. If you are in a group of four and the other three are all sniggering and all have saucy chins, you cannot tell whether they're sniggering partially at you or wholly at each other. Return to **180** and think again.

You write River. Ruby writes River. River has written your name. Gabriel has written your name.

'Now there is a tiebreak,' says your Host. 'You will each get two minutes to convince your fellow Contestants to break the deadlock.'

You have one final choice to stay in. Who should you target to change their mind, Gabriel or River?

What do you do?

- Convince Gabriel to vote for River. Turn to **289**.

- Convince River to vote for Gabriel. Turn to **133**.

'Who was Amrit a threat to?' wonders Rakayah. 'I never heard him saying he thought so-and-so was a Traitor. But he must have, I guess? Or not? Who knows?' Everyone is pottering about, making drinks. Tim tells someone how strong he wants his tea. At this point you'd be disappointed if he didn't.

Teddy has a theory. 'I'm thinking, like, who is Amrit? Or was. Pros and cons. Like, if he was a start-up, would you invest?'

Typical Teddy, you think to yourself. He warms to his theme:

'I liked him. Stand-up guy. But cons? Well, he's never the one who's contributed most to the pot. You know, he's not a Type A. Maybe the Traitors were thinking: we're pretty confident about winning this thing, it's time to get an eye on the end game.'

Deb says she just can't imagine how you could possibly decide the kind of thing the Traitors need to.

'That's the difference between you and me,' says Teddy. 'Probably makes you a better person. But if they're not thinking about the end game now, they ought to.'

Rakayah says that the main thing about Amrit, for her, is that he had a strong interpersonal relationship with Isla. 'It's gotta be something to do with that. 'Cause there aren't really any other one-on-ones, are there?'

'Apart,' Teddy quips to Deb, 'from you and Gregg.'

'Me and Gregg? I suppose. Well, not especially. I do like Gregg. What do you mean?'

'Don't mind me, I'm just messing,' says Teddy, before moving on to more advice he would give the Traitors.

- Turn to **108**.

101

You leave the library and head out into the garden, where you see Isla looking out over the grounds. She turns as you approach.

'Everyone's gone all Agatha Christie in there, haven't they?' she says.

You smile. You have a feeling that she is a lot smarter than she's let on so far, and it would be good to be wary around her.

'Steve-O and David (Henley-upon Thames, 49) are apparently convinced that Luke was murdered because he was a bit dim,' she says.

'Why would the Traitors do that? Surely they'd w&
people in?'

'That's what Alexis (Edinburgh, 39) said!' says Isla. 'It got a bit aw_
ward, to be honest. David wouldn't stop comparing being a pub
landlord to Steve-O being a coastguard. Feels like different stakes
to me. Have you seen Amrit, by the way?'

You shake your head and say your goodbyes.

- Turn to **127**.

102

The atmosphere that night is low. Ruby and Precious sit off on
their own. Tim is quiet with his own thoughts. Gregg looks on
the verge of tears.

River is pretty subdued, as are Gabriel and Gregg, and you suppose you must come across like that too. At this stage, every single
Traitor left makes it so much more likely the Faithfuls will lose. It
occurs to you that you haven't even told anyone the Traitors tried
to seduce you last night and you turned them down. But it feels
like the wrong time. Everyone has enough on their plate with what
just happened.

As you lie in bed, you wonder, briefly, if there will be a murder
tonight. It would be a shame to make it so far, only to fall at the
penultimate fence. But you feel proud of the fact you're still here
at all. What will be will be. You are woken by the sound of the hot
water pipes creaking into life and you smile with relief. You made it.

- Turn to **65**.

You continue around the Castle with River, both of you lost in your thoughts, when you come across Tim, Gabriel and Teddy sitting outside in the sun.

'What ho!' says Tim, jovially. (You sometimes wonder if he has any other mode.)

They squint up at you as you all speculate about what the Mission might be today. A few times, Deb or Nina's names come up in passing and you try to gauge River's reaction without making it obvious. She doesn't seem to react in any noticeable way, but then, thinking about it, you really wouldn't want to play poker against River. She has a very friendly, sunny disposition but it's like a force-field. After a while, you say you're going inside and River says, 'I'm going to hang about out here a bit longer I think,' and smiles breezily at you.

- Turn to **164**.

'You know, Gabriel, until last night,' you say, 'not in a million years. But then Nina *and* Tim? I'm not saying I'm totally agreeing on Anna. But I'm not ruling it out either.'

'That's exactly how I feel,' says Gabriel. 'Let's both just keep an eye on her.'

You nod.

Then word comes around that it's time for the Mission, so you head out into the corridor, where your Host addresses you from the stairs.

'Right, time for you to join together, Faithful and Traitor, and complete today's Mission.'

- Turn to **252**.

105

You walk peacefully, crunching over gravel, as you breathe in the warm late morning air. Someone else clearly has the same idea, as Alexis (Edinburgh, 39) joins you.

'Lovely, isn't it?'

You nod.

'The peace as much as anything else. I've just spent twenty minutes being lectured at by David (Henley-upon-Thames, 49) and Steve-O. Clearly lovely blokes but they both have a lot to say for themselves on why Luke was murdered. Steve-O because he's a coastguard. And David because he's . . . well, he worked behind a bar.'

You pull a wincing face.

'Yes, I think we were all thinking the same thing. Anyway, their grand theory is that Luke was a bit dim, so they killed him.'

You go to speak.

'I know, I know. That's what I said. Why would they make the team stronger by getting rid of dead wood? But you know what men of a certain age are like.'

You walk together in silence for a while, the only sound birdsong and the trees moving in the wind. 'You know who is clever?' she says, apropos of nothing. 'That Elif.'

You make a non-committal face and then you both turn back towards the Castle.

You are all gathered together out in front of the Castle and your Host is smiling broadly.

'So, it's time to stop wondering who isn't on your side, and all take the same side. It's time for today's Mission.'

- Turn to **48**.

106

As you head further into the Castle, you hear voices and put your head around the drawing room door, where Anna and Tim, who feel like an unlikely pair, are sitting next to each other on a sofa, their heads together in concentration. Sitting opposite them, River and Jorge are watching with apparent amusement and Jorge beckons you over. Thinking that you really need to start to get to know him better, you walk over.

'Listen to this, our resident maths experts are deep in debate,' he says.

It transpires that Anna is confused by why anyone would murder Laure.

'It just doesn't make sense in the model,' she says. 'It's not logical.'

'And that's what I'm saying,' says Tim. 'Your model doesn't take into account people behaving illogically or selfishly, or stupidly. What if Laure was a threat in a way that you couldn't see. Or what if they just irrationally didn't like her. Or what if they couldn't decide on who they should murder, so they just picked someone they could all agree on. Also, some people are lying, deliberately introducing errors to the system. At this stage, there's so much bad data flying about the place, I don't think the Traitors could behave rationally if they tried!'

You can't help agreeing with Tim, but you are surprised he's so willing to be seen to be imagining himself as a Traitor.

'What do you think?' says Jorge, looking at you.

What do you do?

- Agree with Tim's theory. Turn to **280**.

- Sit on the fence. Turn to **126**.

107

Oh dear! Have another think, because you've broken the laws of mathematics. Return to **96** and try again.

MISSION

ROGUES' GALLERY

You need: pencil and paper, a bowl, phone with timer

One person* cuts or tears the paper into pieces and writes some names on the pieces. Here are some suggestions, but you can choose your own . . .

Guy Fawkes

Cruella de Vil

Scar (*The Lion King*)

Judas Iscariot

Poison Ivy

Peter 'Wormtail' Pettigrew

Ursula (*The Little Mermaid*)

* If everyone wants to play, you can get each team to write down names for the other team to guess.

The Wicked Witch of the West

Brutus

Baron Greenback (*Danger Mouse*)

Edmund (*The Chronicles of Narnia*)

Darth Vader

. . . as well as the names of two or three of your group. You should fold each slip to hide the writing, then put them in the bowl. Divide into two teams of roughly equal size and hand the bowl to any random player.

Start a 30-second timer. The player with the bowl takes a piece of paper and tries to get the rest of the team to say the name written on it. Any clues are OK except for names. If the player is successful, he or she keeps the piece of paper and pulls out another. If a name is unguessed when time is up, the piece of paper goes back in the bowl and play passes to the other team.

When all the names have been guessed, count how many pieces of paper each team has kept to reveal the winning side.

Then replace the names in the bowl and play using the same names again, with only three words (again, not names) allowed on each turn.

Finally, play it one more time but with only gestures and miming (no words) allowed.

As the Mission finishes, you are in the corridor, and the name on everyone's lips is Isla's.

What do you do?

- See where Isla is and who she's with. Turn to **27**.

- See who else you can have a conversation with. Turn to **119**.

109

You chip in defending Tim, admitting that while you have heard his name a few times today, you've heard Anna's just as often. You can see from the way that Gabriel, Gregg and River are nodding along that you made the right call. Tim has made it a straight popularity contest and he's almost certainly going to win. At this stage, you definitely don't want to get caught voting against the room. Ruby harrumphs and Precious sits there with her arms crossed, but then it's time for the vote.

As the names are revealed, Anna, Ruby and Precious all vote for Tim, restating their original reasoning, but the rest of you vote for Anna. River goes first and says, 'I just didn't hear that passion when you were defending yourself that I'd expect if you were a Faithful.' Everyone else gives some version of that too.

Your Host steps forwards. 'Let's see if you've got it right. Anna, please tell the room, are you Faithful or a Traitor?'

She stands in front of you with a calm smile on her face.

'The numbers never lie. I am a Faithful.'

There is a collective groan. 'I told you,' says Ruby in disgust.

YOU HAVE BANISHED A FAITHFUL.

- Turn to **102**.

110

DAY 2

When you enter the breakfast room, there are already several people at the table. You are starving but wonder if it looks 'wrong' to pile your plate up with food. After all, one of your fellow Faithfuls will not be joining you that morning.

However, you note that this doesn't seem to have stopped Laure (Zurich, 31), who is explaining that as a personal trainer she has to be constantly eating protein. In her case this means ten sausages. Anna is holding forth on the different risk profiles of scrambled and poached eggs. Amrit and Isla are leant forwards, laughing intensely at something. Nina is asking Tim how strong he likes his tea, and he says, 'So strong, you could stand a teaspoon up in it, my dear.'

Teddy is explaining to Jorge that normally by this time he's been up for hours to catch the Asian crypto markets, and Jorge is smiling a large smile with his very beautiful teeth, but clearly has no idea what Teddy is talking about. So many new names and faces to pay attention to.

'So how are you feeling about it all, then?' says Anna, turning and looking at you intently.

What do you do?

- Play up your emotions. After all, no one likes a cold fish. Turn to **184**.

- Keep your cards close to your chest; people can sense it when someone is being fake. Turn to **201**.

111

You cross to Rakayah and lay a friendly hand on her arm. You're joined by River, Anna and Deb. 'It's a shock, isn't it?' offers River.

'Yeah, of course it is, of course,' splutters Rakayah. 'First David and then Alexis too. I just feel like two innocents have carried the can because we have no clue.'

'I hear what you're saying,' says Anna, 'but statistically David was more likely than most of us to either be murdered or banished. And Alexis has always been high odds based on her interaction patterns.'

Rakayah's face brightens. 'You've worked out odds on all of us?'

'Wait, what?' echoes Deb. 'I mean, I won't ask what odds anyone's got on me,' she observes. 'Don't need to. I know I'm a Faithful. Those odds are one hundred per cent.'

Anna is stony faced. 'I'm an actuary. This is what I do. Numbers are the tool but it's actually about people. Before you ask, I've decided I won't be sharing my data. But if it's any consolation, Rakayah, David was a goner from the moment he lied to us.'

A pause, then everyone bursts into laughter. It's clearly a relief after the tension had been building.

'Any consolation!' chuckles Rakayah.

Anna smiles but she doesn't seem to get why everyone's laughing.

- Turn to **188**.

112

As you enter the drawing room, the first to introduce herself is Anna (Whitley Bay, 72), who says she's an actuary. No one really seems to know what that is. 'Is it like an accountant?' you offer. The answer is yes and no, apparently. 'It's about understanding risk. Everyone always thinks it's about numbers, but it's actually about people, so you can see why I think I'll be good in here.' You don't exactly see, and ask her name again. 'Sorry,' you say, 'so many new names'; her name is provided by Jorge (Folkestone, 60), a dentist who seems to be able to remember everyone's names and details pretty much immediately. He smiles at you a lot, then you notice that he smiles at everyone a lot.

A little later, Luke tells you that he bets he's worse with names than you are. You hadn't meant you were bad with names, only that there were so many, but it doesn't seem worth explaining the difference. 'I'm a quantity surveyor,' he says, as if that explains it. 'Oh,' you reply. Then you worry a little that your response might have seemed uninterested, so you add an 'I see.' Also in this group is Nina, but all you get out of her is that she's a 'retired florist'.

They all seem OK. It's hard to process so many first impressions. But you want to meet as many people as you can, so you leave the drawing room and head for the hall.

- Turn to **43**.

113

DAY 12

You find yourself oddly hungry at breakfast, arriving third with Gabriel and River already chatting away. It feels strange for there to be no tension over who arrives this morning. You had become so used to the combination of breakfast and drama.

River says, 'I wonder why they did this. God, you could drive yourself mad, couldn't you? Is there some sort of sneaky ulterior motive at work? I'm just glad we're all here this morning!'

Your host enters and addresses you. 'Good morning. I trust you slept well. A reminder that today is the final day. After the final Round Table, if you are confident there are no remaining Traitors, simply tell me and we will end the game. Either when there are three finalists left or you unanimously decide, the game will end. But if there is even a single Traitor amongst you, the Traitors will win. Until then, do try and relax.'

As you leave the breakfast room, you see Gabriel heading off purposefully down the corridor, whereas River and Ruby are heading towards the door to the garden.

What do you do?

- Head after Gabriel. Turn to **243**.

- Head outside with River and Ruby. Turn to **81**.

114

The less Gregg knows, the less prepared he'll be. And that's useful to the Traitors.

'I wouldn't worry about it,' you say. 'We're all a bit bruised by last night. I think most people, if they think anything about it, just think that you're sensitive.'

'What, even Ruby?' he says.

You're unable to hide the look on your face.

'Thank you,' he says. 'I really appreciate you trying to make me feel better. It's a very kind thing to do.'

Up ahead, Gabriel calls back, 'Everyone's going to play a game in the library!' You both quicken your pace to catch up with the others.

- Turn to **240**.

'And then there were six,' says your Host. 'You have made it this far. But whose race is run? Tonight you must banish another. Let the games begin.'

River is straight out of the blocks. 'I never normally go first but I really have to tonight. I haven't really felt able to talk to many people today. But I think in a way that might have helped me get perspective on some things. And Tim, you know how much I like and respect you, but after last night, with Anna, it just feels like the room went with our hearts, not our heads.' You have to hide your astonishment and keep your face neutral.

Tim is smiling but he sags a little.

Ruby chips in. 'Well, you all know what I'm going to say, but it's absolutely clear to me who is a Traitor and it's Tim. I tried to show you yesterday but you went with Anna and we banished another Faithful.'

Tim is smiling genially but it looks a bit forced this time. He tries to say that, to his mind, murdering Precious would have been the perfect move for Ruby to make to point the finger away from herself. River is nodding tentatively and Gabriel looks thoughtful too.

After last night Tim as a Traitor still makes a lot of sense to everyone. And where his niceness once seemed like his superpower, suddenly, without it, there are a few examples of people remembering him acting in a way that doesn't quite add up. Gregg chips in with a couple of key examples and now Tim's smile almost entirely falls away under the pressure. Ruby is like a star barrister and keeps him under relentless scrutiny. And like a bad witness, he crumbles. He is hostile and patronising and seems to be flailing around trying to blame everyone. First Gregg, then Ruby, then even River. But nothing lands.

As the names are revealed, Tim votes for Ruby, but the rest of you vote for Tim.

Your Host steps forwards.

'Let's see if you've got it right. Tim, are you Faithful or a Traitor?' By this time he's regained his composure somewhat.

'Well, everyone, it's truly been a pleasure getting to know every single one of you . . .' Is it you, or does he linger on Gregg and River for longer than anyone else? You think you see something that looks like disappointment.

'But I have to tell you . . . I'm a Traitor.'

Ruby screams and the whole room lets out its breath.

YOU HAVE BANISHED A TRAITOR.

- Turn to **63**.

You wander over to the lake where you find Amrit and Isla gazing out over the water. You nod to them both.

Isla has her theories about David's banishment and Alexis's murder. You feel compelled to say again how shocked you are, then worry for a bit that you'd already done that enough earlier.

'We've got to try and remember that they're separate though,' says Isla, 'banishments and murders. Even though to us, they're both just gone. David was lovely, but he really got himself tied up in knots with the pub thing. Everyone was looking for something to latch on to, and once he'd confessed, it was only going to go one way.' You realise that you have assumed Isla is a vague, hippy type because of her connection to new age therapy. But she's clearly very sharp-eyed. You make a mental note to pay more attention to her.

'Yeah, totally,' reckons Amrit. 'And so far, anyone who is too obviously investigating has been taken out by the Traitors.'

'So that's your strategy,' giggles Isla. 'Tactical stupidity.'

'Hey!' says Amrit, laughing.

You've noticed that the pair are already close enough that they tease each other.

'Pretty soon, though,' says Isla, 'they're going to have to start getting rid of some good eggs. Because if a Traitor goes up against one of those at any point, they're toast.'

'Egg on toast,' you say. 'That's what I should have had for breakfast.' But everyone just looks at you.

You bid your goodbyes and walk back towards the Castle.

- Turn to **301**.

117

You decide to match Gregg's jovial tone. You chuckle and say that while you won't miss hearing about Laure's healthy breakfasts and glamorous clients, you'll certainly miss her. And you certainly didn't want someone to murder her!

'Someone . . .' says Gregg. 'Seriously, though, guys, that felt like a tipping point last night. We can't banish another Faithful.'

'Too right,' says Rakayah.

You nod forcibly but notice a few people seem to be holding back from speaking freely with you there. You say goodbye and move on.

- Turn to **6**.

118

You make your way into the Round Table, everyone exchanging smiles after a particularly collegiate day. You notice that River still has a daisy in her hair.

'OK, you did well last night,' says the Host. 'You dispatched a Traitor. But can you do the same tonight? Will your deduction skills be up to the task? Let's see!'

Clearly no one wants to go first. You watch Gregg intently, wondering if he has already told others in the group his big secret.

Then he tells the room what he told you earlier, pretty much word for word.

There is a stunned silence. Nina looks carefully controlled but is clearly furious.

'Thanks for your "honesty", Gregg,' she says, making the most aggressive air quotes you've ever seen. 'But if we are being honest, that's not all we talked about, is it? I asked your advice on the best time to tell everyone because I felt bad for lying, and you said that Round Table was the best time. Except now you've told everyone first, making me look terrible.'

Gregg explains that he was going over and over it in his head and then he'd talked to you about it and you'd told him to be completely transparent.

That's exactly the sort of thing the room has jumped on in the past, so it might be wise to act fast.

On the other hand, are Gregg and Nina successfully making this a straight fight between them to be banished, so best to just leave them to it?

What do you do?

- Jump in at this point to frame things for the room. Turn to **219**.

- Let them squabble. Why draw fire unnecessarily? Turn to **271**.

It's another fine day outside and on the garden benches you find Laure, Rakayah, Teddy and Anna.

Teddy is in full flow. 'You just have to think, like, who benefits from it? What are the moves within the moves, you know?'

Rakayah is nodding but with a slightly glazed look on her face.

'And all you can be is yourself,' says Teddy. 'That's all you can truly know. Yourself from the inside out.'

'What, like gut health?' says Rakayah. She looks at him pointedly.

'No, like Isla this morning,' he says. 'Everyone was expecting her to be all boo-hoo about Amrit getting murdered, but she was all like, I'm not gonna fake a response because it's what you expect.'

'I'm afraid I have to disagree with you there, Teddy,' cuts in Anna. 'I found it creepy.'

'It was, wasn't it?' offers Rakayah. 'I think I was probably more shocked about Amrit than Isla was.'

'What about you, Laure?' wonders Teddy. 'Surely you must've been trying to pick up on your ESP-not-ESP thing this morning?'

Laure smiles at the description. 'Yes, you're right, Teddy,' she replies. 'But I agree with you. Isla wasn't giving off bad energy. Someone is, though. And you know what? I feel like I'm gonna have a breakthrough real soon.'

- Turn to **148**.

As you pass the library, someone calls out for you to come and play.

BONUS GAME

THE QUEEN'S DRUMMERS

You need: phone with a stopwatch

Players: at least five, ideally more

One player is nominated the Queen and leaves the playing area.

The others nominate one player as Chief Drummer. The Chief Drummer plays a rhythm on their body (probably while seated). The rhythm should have a few variations and involve different parts of their body.

Once the other players have managed to match the rhythm, the Queen returns to the playing area and starts the stopwatch.

The Queen now walks around inspecting her Drummers. While she is doing so, the Chief Drummer introduces minor variations: adding or removing some beats, or changing some of the parts of the body used. Other players change their drumming to match.

The Queen's job is to identify the Chief Drummer. A wrong guess adds one minute to her time.

Once the Queen has named the Chief Drummer success-fully, her time is recorded and a new Queen is appointed.

After you've finished your game, you sit chatting until the shout goes around that it's time for Round Table.

- Turn to **131**.

Instead of recounting your theory, you join in with the 'poor old Irwin' chatter.

Teddy looks deep in thought, then says, 'I might feel stupid for saying this later but, you know, Tim a Traitor? Just doesn't track for me.'

There are murmurs of agreement. Then Teddy warms to his theme. 'And, you know, there's something else that doesn't add up for me.'

Everyone turns their heads. 'Well . . .' ventures Teddy, 'I do have to say that if I had been a Traitor I would have worried that murdering Irwin would immediately point the finger of blame in my direction.'

The murmurs of agreement are louder now. 'I mean, I would say that,' he adds, 'but you take the point?'

'That's some smart thinking,' remarks Gabriel.

You're frustrated. If you had mentioned your theory, you figure, you'd be getting some kudos and generally thought of as a smart and useful person. You reassure yourself there's still time and make your excuses, saying that you need to get some air.

Alexis smiles and says she'll join you.

- Turn to **198**.

'You know, Gabriel, until a couple of nights ago, not in a million years,' you say. 'Then Nina happened. I'm not saying I'm totally agreeing on Tim. But I'm not ruling it out either.' You feel proud of your reasoning. River was right, the trick is just to pretend you don't know that you're a Traitor.

'That's exactly how I feel,' says Gabriel. 'Let's both just keep an eye on her.'

You nod.

Then word comes around that it's time for the Mission.

- Turn to **252**.

As you come in from the garden, you see Nina on her own in the corridor.

'Beautiful gardens, aren't they?' she says wistfully. 'So many wonderful borders.'

'Sorry about Luke,' you say.

'Ah,' she says. 'All part of the game. Where are you coming from then?'

You feel immediately that you can talk pretty candidly with her and you're almost sure a lot of the others will intuitively trust Nina. You want to be certain that if you do the same, it'll be based on more than instinct. For now, though, she's an ideal sounding board.

You tell her about the battle for supremacy between the alpha males in the garden, and she shakes her head wryly.

'Men. What are they like? I've been in the library where Irwin is being very air pilot about everything, Gregg (Salford, 29) is spinning his grand theories about the Traitors picking a safe choice, Gabriel (Anglesey, 43) is being adorable and gentle, and that young fellah, Teddy, is telling everyone lots of things about his game theories and his job, which is something to do with crypts?'

'Crypto, maybe?'

'What's that when it's at home?'

'It's an internet thing.'

'Ah yes, that makes much more sense. He doesn't have the hands of a gravedigger.'

- Turn to **293**.

124

As you go back outside into the sunlight, the brightness making your eyes blink, the first person you meet is Deb. She tells you that she's got a good sense for body language, which makes you feel a bit self-conscious, so you make an excuse and talk to Amrit (Armagh, 29). He's a very nattily dressed 'on-street fundraiser'. He and Isla (Isle of Man, 26) have immediately bonded over their shared love of aromatherapy oils. You're not sure how they discovered this. Perhaps by the smell?

Also in the group is Irwin (Carlisle, 41). The main thing you notice about Irwin is that he stands with his legs very far apart. Someone whose name you missed says perhaps that's because he's a pilot, which makes little sense to you. Don't pilots have to sit in confined spaces? Steve-O (Lowestoft, 42) is a coastguard but you notice that he stands much less like he's 'on alert'. You tell yourself to stop overthinking everything.

Then there's Rakayah. She's 'in IT'. Before you can say anything, she adds, 'I know that sounds really boring but, well, I mean, you'd probably find it boring. But I honestly don't.' This elicits an affectionate chuckle from Tim (Cornwall, 53), a park-keeper, who seems to be immediately playing the twinkly-eyed grandfather figure of the wider group, even though he's not actually that old.

Having got to know this group as much as you think you can, you wander inside and over to the hall.

- Turn to **66**.

125

Outside, it has stopped raining and it smells of wet earth and lavender. You perch on the steps, like you did that first day, even though they're slightly damp.

'Poor Gregg,' says River, as you all watch him trudge away through the grounds with the weight of the world on his shoulders.

'Yeah, it's weird, isn't it?' says Ruby. 'Even though Nina was a Traitor, he's taken it hard. Traitor guilt perhaps?'

'Yes, maybe he's feeling guilty about knocking off one of his own,' says Precious.

'That's interesting. On the other hand, I think we were all so shocked that Nina was a Traitor,' says River, taking her shoes off and stretching her toes out. She looks up at you.

'It's such a shock,' you say. 'I can only speak for myself but I certainly didn't have Nina on my list until the lie was revealed. Even now, I can't imagine anyone who's left being a Traitor.' You realise how useful suspicion on Gregg could be. 'He certainly does look sad though doesn't he,' you say.

'Do you remember when we used to fill up all of these steps pretty much,' asks River dreamily. 'Now there's only a few of us rattling around in the Castle.' You all stare into the distance.

'Ok, I'm going to say it just because I have to,' says Ruby. 'Gregg is behaving weirdly. But he's a weird guy. But wouldn't Anna and Tim actually be the perfect Traitors? Tim is basically everyone's fantasy uncle, and has Anna ever even had her name written once? And that was a weird speech last night. Wasn't she a bit too happy about Nina going? That smacks of relief to me.' You check to see if there's any reaction from River but she just laughs, so you do too.

'Lovely Tim?!' says River. But she looks around at everyone as they take a moment and she can see they're taking it seriously. You see her looking like she's considering it too. For the first time you think about what might happen if one of the three of you has to sacrifice the other. Was that the real reason they chose you?

- Turn to **278**.

'Oh God,' you say. 'I think that feels a bit above my paygrade. I can barely do long division without a calculator.' Jorge smiles but doesn't flash as many teeth. You are worried that you have come across as deliberately evasive. 'One thing's for sure, I certainly don't envy those Traitors!' you say, your voice suddenly echoing in the quiet library.

- Turn to **144**.

127

As you walk down the corridor, you hear voices and put your head around the doorway into one of the other rooms. Laure and River are sitting with their heads close together in conversation. You go to turn away but Laure beckons you over. 'No, come in, come in. Sit.'

You bristle a little. Does Laure think you need her permission to sit down? No, of course that's not what she meant. But you're starting to feel you and her wouldn't 'click' in real life.

'We were just talking about how sweet Tim is,' Laure says. 'It seems as if there's a few men who are being very loud about their theories, and his position is that at his age he's basically a mushroom.'

'He's definitely sweet,' says River. 'But I think he's very sharp too. And did you see how Elif writes everything down in her little book?'

You tell them about what you'd heard about Steve-O and Dave in the garden.

You are all gathered together in front of the Castle and your Host is smiling broadly.

'So, it's time to stop wondering who isn't on your side, and all take the same side. It's time for today's Mission.'

- Turn to **48**.

128

Right. Here goes nothing.

'I made the decision when I came in here that I would be entirely myself. One hundred per cent honest. That's who I am. And you've all asked me questions and I've told you what I honestly think. I haven't been guiding anything. I've just been honest. To me that's the mark of a Faithful. I can look you all in the eye and tell you I've been completely truthful.'

When you finish speaking, some people are nodding. But others are looking very sceptical indeed. Looking around, you get a sinking feeling.

Then Alexis chimes in, 'I totally agree. But I know for a fact there are some people who can't say that. Dave, is there anything you'd like to share with the group?'

He looks down at the table, shamefaced. Then it all comes spilling out. How he's lied. How there is no pub and how sorry he is.

Deb and Rakayah look heartbroken. Deb says, 'The one thing I can't stand in life is a liar.' With a growing feeling of relief, you see how it becomes all anyone wants to talk about. You nod along and offer the odd word of agreement, but you sink happily into the background. The conversation leads inexorably to the inevitable question – if he was lying about that, what else might he be lying about. When it's time to write a name, almost everyone, you included, writes down David's name.

He stands in front of everyone.

'Well, David,' says the Host. 'You have been chosen to leave. But are you Faithful or a Traitor?'

'I just want to say again to everyone how sorry I am that I lied. But I'm a Faithful.'

There is an audible gasp and Deb shouts out, 'Nooooooo!'

YOU HAVE BANISHED A FAITHFUL.

- Turn to **308**.

129

As you stay quiet, more and more people begin to come around to the idea that Isla had been behaving 'wrong' since Amrit was murdered. She looks around the room, appealing for support. But you stay looking at the pattern on the table.

Laure loudly remarks that 'Something about this really doesn't sit right with me. I am a very good judge of liars – you have to be when you're working with clients and they tell you they've followed the diet you've set for them. And I don't think Isla is lying. But you're all convincing each other.'

This and Isla's initial attack on Deb definitely seem to have caused some people to pause, but as it is time to vote, she looks like she knows what's coming.

- Turn to **75**.

130

DAY 5

As you walk down the stairs and knock on the breakfast room door, you reflect on the fact that there really is nothing like finding that you haven't been murdered to start your day.

Unfortunately, the feeling doesn't last for long, as you sit down and remember that you're about to have to contemplate the ramifications of someone else having been murdered.

You sit with Laure at breakfast. She is telling you what she would typically be having for breakfast on a normal morning 'as a personal trainer'. You haven't heard of lots of the ingredients and really have no idea how one might go about activating a cashew nut, but you're almost certain that she's basically describing muesli and yoghurt.

As she segues in to her favourite topic – her influential clients who she can't name – you feel a strong sense of déjà vu.

What do you do?

- Keep listening. Turn to **181**.

- Use refilling your juice glass as a pretext to find someone else to talk to. Turn to **246**.

131

'So,' says your Host. 'Yesterday. Another banishment, another Faithful gone. You're really making a habit of this. But the good thing is that tonight you have the chance to break that frankly risible losing streak. Well, what are you waiting for? Get to it!'

You all sit in silence, no one wanting to go first.

'Ok, I'm just going to say it,' says Deb. 'But I've been picking up some really strange body language from Isla.'

'Oh blimey, here we go, again,' says Isla. 'Every time one of us thinks we can read someone, we really confidently banish a Faithful. Can we all maybe agree that none of us has any magic powers? I am Faithful. End of.'

'I'm sorry, babes,' says Rakayah. 'You know I love you, but I feel the same way. You even said that the one person he suspected was you.'

'It was a *joke*,' says Isla. 'Why would I draw attention to that if I was a Traitor? That would be stupid.'

'Just to play devil's advocate,' says Tim. 'If a Traitor were looking to explain that decision, this would be a neat defence.'

'Well, I'm just going to come out and say that I think it's odd for one person to be constantly getting Faithfuls banished based on her magic powers,' says Isla.

You catch Isla's eye and she looks genuinely worried. Should you try and help her, or stay hidden in the background?

What do you do?

- Speak up. Turn to **49**.

- Stay quiet. Turn to **129**.

As you head back inside, you pass by the library, where a few people have the cards out again.

BONUS GAME

CAPTURE THE CASTLE: NINCOMPOOP

You need: deck of cards, phone with timer

Players: Town Crier, plus at least two others

Take from the deck two 2s (the Renegades) and one 6 (the Nincompoop). Then add court cards (king, queen, jack) until there are three more cards than there are players.

One player is the Town Crier and should now read the text below.

I am shuffling the cards, and dealing one to everyone, including myself.

I am now placing the remaining cards face down in a row on the table.

Everyone, look at your card. If you have a 2, you are a

Renegade, come to capture the castle. If you have a 6, you are the Nincompoop. Everyone else is a member of the Royal Family. Place your card face down, close to the three already on the table in a way that makes it clear whose is whose.

When I say, 'Let us dance!', the Masked Ball will commence. Everyone – including me – will close their eyes for a count of eight. During that time, any Renegades must open their eyes and clock each other.

Ready . . . Let us dance! One, two, three, four, five, six, seven . . . eight.

Everyone must open their eyes. The King has heard that there may be a Renegade at his Masked Ball. In five minutes' time, he will have someone placed in the stocks. You have five minutes to debate whom to capture. Any of you may claim to have been assigned any of the identities, Royal Family or Renegade.

Additionally, if there is a Nincompoop, he or she must now turn over their 6 and replace it with a face-down card from the three in the middle. That is his or her role, though he or she doesn't know what's on the card.

The time starts . . . now.

Set the timer, and then when the time is up . . .

After a count of five, we shall all vote. The player or players with the most votes shall be placed in the stocks.

If one or more Renegades is placed in the stocks, the Royal Family shall be declared victorious. If there were no Renegades, the Royal Family shall be declared victorious. In all other situations, the Renegades shall be declared victorious. If you decide that the King should exhibit clemency, you should now agree to each vote for the player on your left, and nobody shall be placed in the stocks.

I shall now make the count of five. One, two, three, four, five.

NB: this game can be combined with other Capture the Castle games in the list of games at the start of the book, so long as the total number of cards is always topped up to three more than the number of players using members of the Royal Family.

- Turn to **106**.

When it is your turn to speak, you address River. 'River, I didn't mean to attack you back there. But it came from passion because I know I am a Faithful.'

You spend so much time addressing your comments to her that you don't leave yourself enough time for Gabriel or Ruby. And River does not seem impressed, even by the end. When she speaks, she addresses mainly Ruby and lays out passionately why she so often feels herself speaking for the group. Because she is so passionately a Faithful.

'Now it is time for you to vote again,' says your Host.

This time, you write River. Ruby changes her mind and votes for you. River has written your name. Gabriel again votes for you.

You step forwards. And your Host asks you to say if you are Faithful or a Traitor.

'I'm so happy to have made it to the end. I've learnt so much here. That's why I'm sorry to say, you've made a mistake. I am a Faithful.' There is a groan as you are led away.

YOU HAVE BEEN BANISHED.

To play this day again, please turn to **113**. Better luck next time!

You make your way into the Round Table, everyone exchanging smiles after a particularly collegiate day. You notice that River still has a daisy in her hair.

'OK, you did well last night,' says the Host. 'You dispatched a Traitor. But can you do the same tonight? Will your deduction skills be up to the task? Let's see!'

Clearly no one wants to go first. You watch Gregg intently, wondering if he has already told others in the group his big secret.

'OK everyone, I've got something I need to get off my chest,' he says. ' And I genuinely am saying this because I don't know what to think. But Nina and I went for a long walk in the gardens this morning and it was all great and then she mentioned something about someone in her office. And I think, office, that's weird. I don't know much about floristry but I don't reckon it's very office-based, so I asked her if that was the back office of the florist shop, and she caught herself and was a bit weird. And then she told me that she was actually only a florist for a couple of years and that for most of her career she worked in investment banking. She quit because she stopped believing in what she was doing but that she was basically a really senior banker. Isn't that a bit messed up?'

There is a stunned silence. Nina is carefully controlled but clearly furious.

'Thanks for your "honesty", Gregg,' she says, making the most aggressive air quotes you've ever seen. 'But if we are being honest, that's not all we talked about, is it? I asked your advice on the best time to tell everyone because I felt bad for lying and you said that Round Table was the best time. Except now you've already told everyone and made me look terrible.'

Precious speaks up to say that something feels off about this whole thing; that she'd never defend someone lying, just that there's something that doesn't smell right here.

Gregg explains that he was going over and over it in his head, and then he'd talked to you about it and you'd told him to tell the group.

'So it was something really big. I *knew* there was something fishy,' says Gabriel, looking at you. This is going to come across like you've been keeping secrets again.

Oh dear. You need to do something. But what? It feels like you can attack either Nina or Gregg.

What do you do?

- Explain that Gregg didn't actually tell you what the secret was, and the fact he hasn't made that clear is really suspect. Turn to **297**.

- Concentrate on Nina's lie as the main issue. Turn to **28**.

135

For no particular reason, other than a final feeling he's the last person who would be a Traitor, you write Gabriel. Ruby writes River. River has written your name. Gabriel has written your name.

You step forwards. And your Host asks you to say if you are Faithful or a Traitor.

'I'm so happy to have made it to the end. I've learnt so much here. That's why I'm sorry to say, you've made a mistake. I am a Faithful.' There is a groan as you are led away.

YOU HAVE BEEN BANISHED.

To play this day again, please turn to **113**. Better luck next time!

136

Through the window of the drawing room, you can see a group with an impressively large cafetiere. You'd skipped coffee at breakfast, so you fancy one now. Alexis is limiting herself to one caffeinated drink a day, so she opts to continue her walk instead.

You join the others in the drawing room. Irwin is not forgotten, but the topic is the perennial: who might have been acting strangely since the Traitors were given their roles?

Rakayah has a theory about Elif. 'You know how she's always writing in that notebook? I don't reckon she was when she arrived. I would have noticed.'

That could be because there was so much to take in at the start, you think, although arguably there is also a lot to write down (if you are a notebook person).

Jorge has a theory that everyone needs to be paying much more attention to who is forming an intense relationship with each other and mentions Isla and Amrit ('the aroma gang'), of course, and makes a joke about River and Rakayah (they're sitting close together on a sofa that's not quite big enough). And, of course, everyone has noticed that Gregg has taken a shine to Deb. Rakayah turns to you.

'What do you think?'

Here is another opportunity for you to take the lead.

What do you do?

- Advance your theories about the Traitors. Turn to **207**.

- Continue to keep your theories to yourself. Turn to **200**.

137

River listens intensely as you explain the various theories flying around on why both she and Tim might be plausible Traitors.

'Interesting,' she says. 'I thought that might be the case after last night. I think Tim might be under too much pressure tonight, whatever we do.'

You try and keep your face impassive. 'I'll go and let Tim know. Take care.'

She excuses herself and says she needs to go and get changed before Round Table. You have ten blissful minutes as you sit with your eyes closed, listening to the tick of a clock, before Gabriel puts his head around the door and says, 'It's time.'

You get up and walk towards the Round Table, your heart beating so loudly in your chest that you think people must be able to hear it.

- Turn to **115**.

138

'I'm sure you've encountered how people experience grief in different ways,' you say, keeping your tone absolutely blank. 'In your day job.'

'Oh, absolutely,' says Gabriel, equally measured. 'Rakayah's certainly been up and down like a yoyo, hasn't she?'

You agree, and wonder what it must feel like to have ordered someone's murder. Might you feel so guilty in the morning that you're driven to tears?

'None of us can know how we'd act until we are a murderer ourselves,' reckons Gabriel. 'What I've been trying to remember is whether Rakayah started acting differently after the Traitors were chosen. But I don't think she did.'

'No. Neither do I,' you say. 'In fact, she was—'

At that moment, at the other end of the table there's a burst of loud laughter and you both crane your necks to try and listen. Deb comes back to sit down, rubbing tears of laughter from her eyes.

'What's so funny?' asks Gabriel.

'So it turns out that Anna is running odds on all of us being banished or murdered. And David was always in trouble, as soon as he told a lie. I told her, you can run any numbers you like on me but I *know* I'm a Faithful.'

- Turn to **84**.

139

What you think you heard Deb say is still on your mind as the group divides into smaller groups. You're with Tim, Jorge and Anna.

And it's at the forefront of your mind when Jorge speculates about alliances. He reminds you sometimes of the kind of TV detective that keeps track of a case with photographs and documents connected with pieces of string. Except it's all just in his head. He unspools friendships and conflict you hadn't known existed. Isla and Irwin hadn't got on? Who knew!

But then Jorge mentions Nina and Deb. 'Firm friends very fast,' he reckons. 'Something has obviously clicked there.'

It reminds you of what you're almost certain you heard earlier, and you see an opportunity. Last night was too close to disaster again. You don't want to keep having to rely on evasive manoeuvres, if only for your poor heart. Surely if you play this right, it would be all anyone will talk about at the Round Table. Deb is vulnerable because of her unfounded confidence in her reading of body language. Nina is one of the people you have warmed to the most, and you're pretty sure she's not a Traitor (well, as sure as you can be). Do you risk her as collateral damage in an attempt to defend yourself?

What do you do?

- Mention what you think you heard. Turn to **269**.

- Keep it to yourself. Turn to **196**.

140

'I was thinking that earlier,' you say. 'And I'd almost forgotten the stuff with Deb before that. It feels like Gregg's had a real run of dramas, hasn't he?'

River is nodding along. 'Gregg's certainly had a lot of things that have distracted anyone from looking at him, hasn't he?'

Ruby comes out and says, 'Last game in the library before tonight?' And you both head back inside.

- Turn to **288**.

'Well, it's that time again,' says the Host. 'Yesterday, you banished a Faithful. Will you make the same mistake again? Or will you snare a Traitor? Whatever happens, one more of you must leave.'

Looking around the table, it seems as if everyone has their game face on. Yesterday, there was a kind of lightness, as no one quite knew what to expect. You feel calm.

'I'll go first this time,' says Jorge, smiling. 'I know two things. I know that I'm Faithful, and I know we've all been having various conversations. And it's been very interesting to see who has been leading conversations and who has been following them. I just want to throw out two names of people who I feel have been very actively convincing people to see things a certain way. And that's you and *you*.'

You realise that Jorge is pointing at Alexis and you. You feel less calm.

With mounting horror, as others start to chime in, you realise that there is quite a lot of agreement. Several people are saying they've heard both your names a lot today and that you've had big theories. You know how quickly the herd mentality can take hold. You need to do something drastic to take yourself out of the equation.

What do you do?

- Use the secret you know about David and his fictional pub. Turn to **218**.

- Defend yourself but leave out any mention of David. Turn to **128**.

142

You make sure you've got everyone's full attention and announce: 'I didn't have any beef with Laure and I don't think she did with me.'

You pause. You feel you need to say more, but it's not possible to say much about something that's been inflated from nothing. You add that you're not going to pretend you and she were best friends . . . but that makes it sound like there was a problem. You add that there really wasn't anything. Then you repeat that, and regret it. It really does come across as someone protesting too much. Looking at the clock, you realise it's almost time for Round Table.

What do you do?

- Act as confidently as you can. Turn to **4**.

- Try and keep a low profile. Turn to **147**.

143

'You know, Gabriel, until a couple of nights ago,' you say, 'I'd have said not in a million years. She's so Faithful. But then Nina? I'm not saying I'm totally agreeing on River. But I'm not ruling it out either.'

'That's exactly how I feel,' says Gabriel. 'Let's both just keep an eye on her.'

You nod.

Then word comes around that it's time for the Mission.

- Turn to **252**.

144

Before the Mission today, your Host explains that you will now be playing for something extra. The winning group will win the chance to enter the Armoury, where you will have the opportunity to secure something called a 'Shield', which protects the bearer from murder. So far, you wouldn't have had the chance to get a Shield, so you clearly need to up your game. Literally.

MISSION

THE LYING CHEFS

You all file down a grand staircase, through a door, then down a rudimentary staircase past windowless walls.

You're underground now and you can smell soup. 'We'll be going to the kitchen, then,' offers Gregg.

'Been down here before, have you?' asks Deb.

'No,' says Gregg. 'And I'm not being funny but what do you mean by that question?'

'Yeah,' Nina chimes in. 'What do you mean by that? Do you think the Traitors meet in the kitchen or something?'

'Well, I wouldn't know, would I?' insists Deb. 'I mean, sometimes a question is just a question.'

'And sometimes Gregg does something like smelling soup and decides to tell everyone that it's coming from where food is made!' That's River, with an observation delivered like a joke. No one's sure whether it is a joke, but it serves the purpose of diffusing what might have turned into tension. And by now, you can see that Gregg's statement of the obvious was quite right. You're all in the kitchen.

Clusters of garlic dangle from the rafters. You're next to two enormous earthenware pots of rosemary and sage. You whisper to Tim: 'How do they grow indoors, with no windows down here?'

'Who cares?' he replies. This seems out of character. Next to a great wooden table are three chefs, one of whom coughs: a 'your attention, please' kind of a cough.

'These are my colleagues,' she announces. 'And I'm telling you the truth. We really are chefs. But not all of my colleagues always tell the truth. Not everything you're about to hear from these two, Shuggie and Dougie, will be true.'

You all eye Shuggie and Dougie. One's wearing a toque. The other isn't. The one in the headgear announces: 'Nice to meet you all, I'm Dougie.'

'Yep,' adds the other. 'And I'm Shuggie.'

Most of you nod. It makes sense on the face of it.

And then the chef who first spoke pipes up again. 'Tonight, we'll cook you our finest, favourite dishes,' she announces, 'if you can tell us whether Shuggie is wearing a hat or not?'

There's a silence. The nods turn to bewildered sidelong glances.

'And if you can't, it's beans on toast.'

Nina's first. 'We can't know, I guess. Because only she's necessarily telling the truth.'

'Unless,' opines Gregg, 'she's not and that's part of it.'

'It's not part of it,' say about half a dozen voices.

You try to hold two thoughts at the same time: the thought that Nina is right, and the thought that you think you can tell which is which.

Take a moment to think it through, because the solution is below.

Anna's next to have a thought. 'Is it . . . do we decide based on which of them we trust more? Or . . . less?'

'No, that's it,' says Teddy. 'We don't need to. You're right, Anna, we have to mistrust them both. Hear me out, yeah? We know at least one of them is lying because, well, that's part of the puzzle. But it can't just be one of them, 'cause . . .'

'. . . 'cause then they'd both be Shuggie!' Anna again. And then another thought: 'Or Dougie, I guess.'

'Right,' says Teddy. 'So they're both lying. So the one who hasn't got the hat, who said he was Shuggie, is Dougie. So the other one, who has got the hat, is Shuggie. So Shuggie is wearing the hat and we dine like kings tonight!'

The chefs smile.

After the Mission, the winning team are taken down a corridor you haven't noticed before and return excitedly with tales of numbered chests you have to choose from. You ask them if anyone won a Shield, only for Anna to intone, 'It is my strong advice to everyone that we do not share who has won the Shield. That way, if we are lucky, it will act as a potential Shield for anyone in the whole group. Unless a Traitor wins it, of course.' And that is why Anna gets the big bucks as an actuary.

- Turn to **225**.

145

'I'll go first this time,' you say. 'And it was actually something you said earlier, Ruby, that made me think of this.' She has a look of apprehension on her face. 'You said that you had been watching at the moment of banishment in case something stood out. And I suddenly worked out what it was that was bugging me. The night Tim was banished, he gave Gregg a look, a really specific kind of look. It wasn't anger, it was disappointment. The kind you might give a child who had disappointed you, or, perhaps, the more I think about it, a fellow Traitor who had turned on you. All of his behaviour since makes sense as a mixture of shame and caution.'

You watch as Ruby has a look of dawning realisation on her face. River says that she would never have believed it but it makes so much sense.

Gregg keeps an admirably blank face and tries to defend himself, explains that he's basically a simple, straightforward guy and that this has all been too much for him. He tries to say that you are clearly distracting from your own behaviour, but you can see that your theory is stacking up for everyone else.

When the names are written, Gregg votes for you, but everyone else votes for him.

'Well then,' says your Host. 'Let's see whether you got this one right or not. Gregg, are you Faithful or a Traitor?'

'I wasn't lying that I'm a simple guy.'

He looks everyone in the eye, one by one.

'I'm Faithful.'

You make sure to put your head in your hands in anguish. When you look up, River is looking at you with a barely perceptible look of admiration.

YOU HAVE BANISHED A FAITHFUL.

- Turn to **233**.

146

You decide that this is the wrong way to reveal your secret. So you try to come up with a plausible alternative, but your brain is blank and you end up saying something vague about things just being too intense. Even you can hear it sounds weak. River seizes upon that and – even you have to admit – makes a pretty good case for why at this stage in the game everyone has to trust their guts on this stuff.

When it's time for people to hold up names, you vote for River and are gratified to see that Gabriel does too. But everyone else votes for you.

'Well, let's see if you've made the right decision,' says your Host. 'Are you Faithful or a Traitor?'

You take a moment. 'I'm a Faithful,' you say.

YOU HAVE BEEN BANISHED.

To play this day again, please turn to **65**. Better luck next time!

You cast your eyes around the room to see whether anyone is looking at you with what you take to be suspicion. Then you worry that this in itself looks guilty, so try to slump back in your seat. You slump too far and the seat's legs make a noise when you adjust yourself.

Your Host reminds you that you have yet to banish a Traitor, and asks: 'Who would like to start?'

You are nervous that Gregg will raise your beef with Laure. You feel your shoulders sag against your will.

What do you do?

- Jump in before Gregg can start speaking. Turn to **83**.

- Let Gregg speak, making sure you don't look like you're fearful of what he has to say. Turn to **61**.

148

In the corridor you're about to pass Gregg when he whispers to you jovially, 'I see you were finding Laure fascinating company at breakfast?'

You don't like this. You don't want the others being able to read when you're not feeling like the loyal team player the name 'Faithful' suggests.

'Don't worry, she couldn't tell. Guarantee it. Just me. I'm a bit of an amateur body language reader. Not a pro like Deb, of course.'

You wonder to yourself: is Gregg deliberately being snide? Or is he trying to be funny but it's just not coming across very well? He has a kind of pleasant, open demeanour and you had assumed he was basically a simple bloke, but now you're not so sure.

- Turn to **120**.

149

In the library it's cool and quiet. But everything is about ten times as intense. You realise that your moment of choice that night means you're Faithful now, not just by appointment. You feel even more Faithful, if anything. And even more determined that this game does not end badly.

You sink into one of the armchairs, when you're startled by a voice close by.

'Are you hiding too?' asks River. You can't help but jump. 'Sorry,' she says. 'I'm finding it all a bit intense out there. I felt like a game of cards would even be too much. The Mission took it out of me.'

'Yes, it is all getting quite intense, isn't it?' you say.

'I feel like I have no idea what's going to happen tonight,' she says. 'I've ducked out of pretty much every chance to talk to anyone, which isn't like me at all. At the risk of making you do my home-work, what's everyone talking about?'

You think for a moment. It has felt as if the main gossip you've heard has been about Tim or River, herself. Here is an opportunity to potentially load the dice. Should you give her the heads-up about her and Tim? Or keep quiet about it?

What do you do?

- Tell River that people are leaning towards her and Tim. Turn to **3**.

- Be more vague. Turn to **274**.

150

'Oh, I think she's being modest,' you say. 'We certainly discussed it, but I wouldn't say it was *my* idea at all. In fact, thinking about it, I'm pretty sure it was Alexis who raised it in the first place.' The three of them seem disappointed. Well, apart from Gregg, who continues to watch Deb.

At that moment, Teddy puts his head around the door and says, 'It's Round Table time.'

- Turn to **206**.

151

You wander along the corridor, thinking about how only a few days earlier, it was almost impossible to find somewhere that people weren't. But now it feels empty. You aren't entirely sure which you prefer, just that at every stage there have been different challenges.

You listen to the sound of the Castle creaking in the heat of the sun. Out of the window you watch clouds moving over distant hills. Your heart feels like it's been beating at double speed the whole morning, but at least here you can stop worrying you're coming across as a Traitor.

During the Mission, you found yourself constantly checking that this was how you would normally behave. How are River and Tim so effortlessly able to appear calm and normal?

You hear the sound of laughter in the corridor and, when you stick your head around the door, Gabriel says, 'Hooray, come and play a game with us!'

Deep breath, and off you go.

- Turn to **264**.

152

With a flash of inspiration, it all comes together. The image of Rakayah nudging Gregg that morning as you approached. The number of times she was there in the background, guiding conversations. The way that she is so emotional around the murders.

You lay it all out, calmly and reasonably. Not to accuse her, but just to see if others in the room have noticed. You are even magnanimous enough to say that you may well be wrong and it may all be a series of innocent coincidences, but that you have to be honest about what you've noticed. As you finish speaking, you are relieved to see that people are nodding, with expressions of dawning realisation. Rakayah tries to bring it back by pointing out that you are the only one who had genuine beef with Laure. But Gregg pipes up and says, 'Ooh, I don't want to contradict you there, Rak, but I'm pretty sure I made it clear that was always a joke about Laure and breakfast. My fault, I'm sure.'

As people read out the names, several have voted for you. But twice as many have voted for Rakayah. You are barely taking it in as you look around with relief.

Before you know it, Rakayah is standing next to the Host. 'Rakayah, you have been banished, but before you go, it's time to reveal if you're a Traitor or a Faithful.'

'I am a Traitor,' says Rakayah, smiling. At first you think you've misheard. Then the room erupts.

YOU HAVE BANISHED A TRAITOR.

- Turn to **223**.

153

You write Ruby. Ruby writes River. River votes for Ruby. Gabriel votes for Ruby.

'Ruby, you have been banished. Please tell us if you are Faithful or a Traitor.'

She steps forwards. 'I am so proud to have made it this far, even though I rejoined the game late. It's been a pleasure to get to know each and every one of you. But I'm afraid you've made a mistake. I am a Faithful.' You all exclaim in shock as Ruby is quietly led away. You have no idea what this means but suddenly you are full of doubt.

'So,' says your Host. 'The final three. Please step forwards and reveal whether you are Faithful or a Traitor.'

Gabriel steps forwards, smiling. 'When I came in here, I knew I just wanted to be me, whatever else happened. I wanted to be true to myself. And that's why I'm so happy to say that I am a Faithful.' One down!

You step forwards solemnly. 'I'm so happy to have made it to the end. I've learnt so much here. That's why I'm delighted to say, I am a Faithful.' You and Gabriel beam at each other and you turn to River, who has a slightly odd look on her face.

River steps forwards and pauses. 'This game has been one of the most amazing experiences of my life. I've loved meeting everyone. Which is why I'm really sorry to say, I'm a Traitor.'

Everyone but River groans. She just stands there, smiling broadly. You can't believe that River was a Traitor. But, if you think about it, that's the whole point.

THE TRAITORS HAVE WON.

To play this day again, please turn to **113**. Better luck next time!

154

'Although,' you say. 'I really don't know. All I know is that this is going to test us all, isn't it?' Not the greatest insight, but hopefully not one that anyone can disagree with too strenuously. And perhaps it's good to not raise your head above the parapet. After all, there are Traitors among you who are looking for threats to themselves.

You nod along for a little while as others advance their grand theories, before the gong sounds and it's time to head up for bed.

- Turn to **259**.

155

'They got one of the good eggs,' wails Isla.

Your Host enters. 'As many of you will no doubt have worked out, last night Amrit was murdered.'

The general mood is subdued. It's not a morning of outrage, more bafflement. 'Why Amrit?' wonders Gregg. River and Gabriel make a beeline for Isla, who will be getting a fair share of hugs. She looks blank. Shock, you reckon. You haven't made a one-to-one connection like Amrit and Isla had, so you don't feel you can put yourself in her shoes.

A tiny voice in the back of your head says that if you were a Traitor, then murdering your best mate would be a hell of a way to put everyone off the scent. But mentioning that would be a very high-risk strategy as Isla is so popular.

What do you do?

- Sit down with Teddy, Deb and Rakayah. Turn to **100**.

- Join the gang around Isla. Turn to **291**.

BONUS GAME

CAPTURE THE CASTLE: IMPOSTOR

You need: deck of cards, phone with timer

Players: Town Crier, plus at least two others

Take from the deck two 2s (the Renegades) and one 9 (the Impostor). Then add court cards (king, queen, jack) until there are three more cards than there are players.

One player is the Town Crier and should now read the text below.

I am shuffling the cards, and dealing one to everyone, including myself.

I am now placing the remaining cards face down in a row on the table.

Everyone, look at your card. If you have a 2, you are a Renegade, come to capture the castle. If you have a 9, you are the Impostor. Everyone else is a member of the Royal Family.

Place your card face down, close to the three already on the table in a way that makes it clear whose is whose.

When I say, 'Let us dance!', the Masked Ball will commence. Everyone – including me – will close their eyes for a count of eight. During that time, any Renegades must open their eyes and clock each other.

Ready . . . Let us dance! One, two, three, four, five, six, seven . . . eight.

Everyone must open their eyes. When I say, 'Is there an Impostor?', we will all again close our eyes for a count of eight. During that time, the Impostor may take for themselves any card on the table and replace it with their own, or may choose not to.

Ready . . . Is there an Impostor? One, two, three, four, five, six, seven . . . eight.

Everyone must open their eyes. The King has heard that there may be a Renegade at his Masked Ball. In five minutes' time, he will have someone placed in the stocks. Your identity is the one on the card in your place, regardless of what you started with. You have five minutes to debate whom to put in the stocks. Any of you may claim to have been assigned any of the identities Royal Family, Renegade or Impostor.

The time starts . . . now.

Set the timer, and then when the time is up . . .

After a count of five, we shall all vote. The player or players with the most votes shall be placed in the stocks.

If one or more Renegades is placed in the stocks, the Royal Family shall be declared victorious. If there were no

Renegades, the Royal Family shall be declared victorious.
In all other situations, the Renegades shall be declared
victorious. If you decide that the King should exhibit
clemency, you should now agree to each vote for the player on
your left, and nobody shall be placed in the stocks.

I shall now make the count of five. One, two, three, four, five.

NB: this game can be combined with other Capture the
Castle games in the list of games at the start of the book,
so long as the total number of cards is always topped up to
three more than the number of players using members of
the Royal Family.

• Turn to **217**.

Along the corridor there is a door you haven't noticed before. It opens and you walk up a steep stone spiral staircase. So this is where the Conclave is!

You enter a dark chamber high in the rafters of the Castle. Waiting for you in the room are two shadowy figures. You can barely take the tension as they slowly pull their hoods back.

'Surprise!' say Tim and River.

You are so full of questions but there is no time for detailed conversation. Tim explains that they recruited you because of how you played the Nina and Gregg situation that night. They were sure you'd be an asset. The main thing, whatever you do, is to not change your behaviour.

'Just keep calm, and keep thinking of yourself as a Faithful,' says River, squeezing your arm. 'It gets so even you start to believe it.'

You are taken back down to your room where you try and sleep, your mind churning.

YOU ARE A TRAITOR.

- Turn to **5**.

158

'That's the trick,' says your Host. 'It's designed to look as if there's information missing. But it's not information you need to answer the question.' Return to **228**.

159

As soon as you open your mouth, all eyes fall on you. Of course, you say to yourself immediately. You make what you think is a decent case: you say that it's too early to have a plan, that surely only the Traitors have a plan already.

You wonder if you're starting to gabble. So you stop. It's at this point that Laure says that you haven't explained why you felt nervous. You say that you hadn't needed to, because you weren't nervous. But you're acutely aware that you sure sound nervous now, and everything you try to do makes you sound more nervous.

Gregg (the other apparently nervous one) seems to have been forgotten.

As the names start to be held up, it's clear that it will be between you and Rakayah. Gregg receives one single vote.

You and Rakayah are on equal votes when you realise that Laure is the last one to cast her vote and that your fate is sealed.

As you stand up and prepare to let them know that yet again they have banished a Faithful, it is little comfort.

YOU HAVE BEEN BANISHED.

To play this day again, please turn to **31**. Better luck next time!

160

'Well, here we are,' your Host says. 'By the end of the day, we'll know whether it is the Faithfuls or the Traitors who have won the game. But first you must choose one of you to be banished now. So go to it!'

You all look around the room, everyone waiting for someone else to go first but no one wanting to break the silence. You decide that you are going to go first, rather than run the risk of someone else pointing the finger at you. But what is the right angle to take? You have to try and forget what you know and imagine yourself in their heads. What are Gabriel, Gregg and Ruby most likely to believe? You make the decision that you have a much better chance of winning the game with River still in it and just pray that she feels the same. But what about the others?

Ruby has been such an active presence since she came back to the Castle. But if she were a Traitor, she'd effectively have taken out two of her own. Surely there'd have been visible bad blood there? Would the boys believe that?

Gabriel? It would be quite high risk, but equally, Tim and Nina's banishments mean there is a way of making it potentially sound plausible.

You know for a fact that there are doubts brewing about Gregg. Out of everyone, he feels like potentially the one that most would gather around.

What do you do?

- Throw doubt about Ruby. Turn to **86**.

- Question whether anyone can be as nice as Gabriel seems to be. Turn to **44**.

- Point the spotlight at Gregg. Turn to **145**.

161

It's tempting to believe this but it's not true. It may have been true, but now that you know that nobody in the groups of three or four said that they could tell, you have new information. And it's actually immensely helpful. Return to **180** and have another go.

162

This is going badly for you. Try using some coins or something, slide them across the table. Return to **96** and try again.

163

'Oh gosh,' you say. 'I don't know. All I know is that this is really going to test us all, isn't it?' Not the greatest insight, but hopefully not one that anyone can disagree with too strenuously. And perhaps it's good to not raise your head above the parapet. After all, there are Traitors among you who are looking for threats to themselves.

You nod along for a little while as others advance their grand theories, before the gong sounds and it's time to head up for bed.

- Turn to **259**.

164

Inside, you walk past the drawing room where you hear Gregg saying, 'It's all very silly really. I write these novels about a police officer with a secret. Nothing that would be helpful here. I don't know why I didn't mention it.'

Then you hear Deb's voice saying, 'Oh totally. It's not really a lie, is it, more just leaving out saying something.' You linger in the corridor to hear more, but then it's time to head outside for today's Mission.

- Turn to **168**.

You take your seats, then there is a long pause. Everyone eyes each other. It seems for a moment as if Irwin is looking at you. Steve-O seems to have his game face on.

'So here we are,' says your Host. 'Your first Round Table. Will you banish a Traitor, or will a Faithful suffer at your hands? Whatever happens, you must discuss and then vote, together.'

From everything you've heard, there are some big theories flying about. Who knows what will happen next.

As usual, Tim is smiling amiably. You idly wonder what would happen if he accused someone. He is one of the few people you haven't heard anything even slightly negative about. You catch his eye and give him an expression that you hope reads, 'This is crazy.'

A moment, then he gives you an expression that you're pretty sure means something like, 'I know, right?', so you think you're OK.

Tim breaks the ice.

'Well, I'll go first. The thing is,' he says, 'we haven't actually got a lot to go on. Or much that's concrete, at any rate. I wonder whether—'

'Yes, Tim,' interrupts Laure, 'you're one hundred per cent right, we've got to go with our emotions. I'm lucky, 'cause I trust my heart more than my head, you know?'

Gregg asks: 'Right, so what does your heart say?'

'That's just it: I dunno.' She laughs at how this sounds. 'Except that I don't think a Traitor would ask me that, you know?'

It certainly would be a bold move on Gregg's part, you're thinking to yourself, when Teddy pipes up.

'Except we do have a lot to go on. Right? It's about understanding game theory and basic psychology.'

Steve-O looks sceptical. 'Seriously, you're not saying you can tell by looking at someone whether they're a Traitor or not. 'Coz—'

'That is just what I'm saying,' insists Teddy. His tone is super-serious. It's so serious, in fact, that it makes River giggle, but she quickly suppresses it. Unfortunately, that makes you want to laugh too, but you maintain your poise.

'Would you let me, though?' asks Teddy.

Nina says: 'What, look at us? I mean, sure, you're looking at us.'

'No,' says Teddy, 'I mean really look at you. One at a time.'

You think you hear another suppressed giggle, possibly from Amrit.

'I'm gonna do it. Ready?'

It seems terribly quiet all of a sudden.

So Teddy starts. He fixes his gaze on River, who's immediately to his left. She eyes him back completely blankly. Most people do. You make a mental note of who doesn't; it's going to take a bit of time to get to you. Rakayah can't really keep eye contact. Tim has what seems to you an uncharacteristic frown, not so twinkly now. Nina looks back at Teddy briefly, almost in challenge, then down in her lap.

And before you know it, Teddy's about to stare you straight in the face. Just as he does, your urge to laugh returns. You're worried that if it comes out, you might look disrespectful. You're also worried that if you try to suppress it, you'll look like you've got something to hide.

What do you do?

- Quickly let out a little snort and then look back at Teddy calmly. Turn to **187**.

- Purse your lips and try to suppress your laughter. Turn to **190**.

166

'I want to say that I know Gregg has been spinning tales about me,' you say, as Gregg's face falls. 'But all of you who know me know that I don't have a problem with anyone. So the only explanation I can come up with is that Gregg is distracting us from paying attention to him. Who else but a Traitor would behave like that?'

As you finish speaking, you realise you have made a mistake. People are frowning and shaking their heads.

'I'm sorry,' says River, 'but that just doesn't ring true to me. I've never heard Gregg introducing rumours about anyone. He's made a few jokes and he certainly joins in, but Gregg as puppet master just doesn't work for me.'

One by one, people chime in to agree and you realise you've committed the cardinal sin of being mean to a puppy. To make it even worse, Gregg looks at you and apologises. 'I'm just so sorry that I've made you feel like that.'

There's a bit of back and forth on a couple of pet theories. Tim theorises that no one can possibly be as nice as Gabriel seems. In response, Gabriel says he's still suspicious of Deb's ideas on body language leading the room previously. But nothing else really takes hold. As the time comes to reveal the names on the slates, it is over-whelmingly your name that is held up.

Before you know it, you are standing next to your Host, who is telling you, 'It's time to reveal if you're a Traitor or a Faithful.'

'I am a Faithful,' you say, your voice flat, disappointed at yourself as much as anything else.

You hear sharp intakes of breath and wails of frustration as you leave the room.

YOU HAVE BEEN BANISHED.

To play this day again, please turn to **283**. Better luck next time!

167

You leave the drawing room and head out towards the welcoming bright sunlight of the back door. As you reach the steps, you see Ruby heading towards you, and River walking off towards the lake. They've obviously been enjoying a stroll in the sunlight.

'Hallooo,' you call. Ruby is slightly out of breath as she reaches you.

'River and I just found the most incredible walled garden back there,' she says. 'There's strawberries and lettuces, loads of delicious looking stuff.' You both sit down on the steps.

'Well, Gabriel and I are stumped,' you say after a few seconds.

'River and I were literally just saying that,' says Ruby. 'I thought I'd be smart and watch really closely how people acted at the last couple of banishments, but I didn't spot anything. You try and think back, to see if there's anything that stands out. But who knows what normal behaviour is in such an abnormal situation.'

You chat for a bit about how weird it is that at least one of the five of you is a Traitor, and how this has changed what you think about how people lie. You had both previously thought you were good judges of whether someone is lying, but you've realised that you're not at all.

As you're sitting there, Gregg joins you. 'Phew, it's like the *Mary Celeste* in there. For a while I thought I was the only one left and that was all part of it. I started getting a bit panicky.'

After a few more minutes you decide to head back inside and see if you can find the others. It's almost time for the last Mission.

- Turn to **276**.

MISSION

WHAT ARE YOUR WORDS WORTH?

You need: pencils and paper

Players: three or more

In 'What Are Your Words Worth?', the letter A is worth 1 point, B is worth 2, C is worth 3 . . . all the way to Z, which is worth 26.

The oldest player names a category (such as Countries) and players secretly write down something that fits that category (so Zimbabwe would be worth 81 but Chad only 16).

The oldest player either declares that they believe they have the highest scoring of all the words or phrases played by saying 'highest' (though they might be bluffing), or says 'pass'. Play passes to the left.

Each player can then pass (and withdraw from competing in the category), or claim that their word is higher scoring (they too might be bluffing) by saying 'higher'.

If a claim to have the highest scoring word goes unchallenged, that player reveals their word. So long as it fits the category, that player gets a point.

If two or more players persist in claiming to have higher scoring words than each other, they all reveal what they have. So long as the word that actually has the highest score fits the category, its player gets a point and all other players lose a point.

> **Variant with *more* bluffing:** *Use toothpicks to indicate your confidence; other players must match you or go higher.*

> **Variant with *no* bluffing:** *Players simply reveal their words and the point goes to the highest scoring answer, so long as it fits the category.*

Tip: While X, Y and Z might not be the most useful letters, R, S and T score relatively well and are pretty common in English-language names and phrases.

After the Mission, the winning team head off to the Armoury and you realise that being good at Missions is going to be much more important from now on.

- Turn to **139**.

You head out with everyone else, aware of how you're walking, what you're doing with your hands.

You end up sitting with River and Tim as they discuss horoscopes. You desperately want to talk to them but you're too exposed and anyone could walk by.

'I've just never understood how everyone could possibly be one of twelve things,' says Tim. 'And it's always "Geminis are very friendly but can be unfriendly if wronged, so they have their cake and eat it." ' River is fanning herself with a straw hat, smiling.

'I sometimes doubt we really even need twelve,' says River, laughing. 'I think I could put all my exes into one group.' The three of you chat for a bit longer, as you try desperately to think of how you would have acted in this context, before you allowed yourself to be seduced.

Both of them say they're too hot and head inside, but you stay outside, grateful for the moment to yourself. A couple of minutes later, Gabriel comes and sits next to you. For a moment you get a flash of panic that he is so sensitive he will just know you're a Traitor, but he seems to be behaving completely normally.

'Want to hear Ruby's latest theories?' he asks. You nod and he leans in. 'So, you, me and Gregg seem to have somehow snuck through because of stupidity, niceness and just general trustworthiness. But she's not so sure about River and Tim. What do you think?' You can't defend both of them, it would look too suspicious.

Between River and Tim, who would it be better to point the finger at? You think carefully about how to respond.

- Agree she might be onto something with River. Turn to **14**.

- Say that Tim is where your suspicions lie. Turn to **122**.

170

This is a very odd thing to think, as we know that the people in the groups of two found it incredibly easy to tell. Return to **180** and have another think.

171

'Well, I don't think you're one, and I know I'm not!' announces Alexis airily when you're on your own. You both laugh.

'I think you're spot on by the way,' she says. 'There's no way the Traitors would be stupid enough to bump someone off who was threatened by them so directly like that.'

'I just think we need to start getting into the heads of the Traitors more.' Alexis is nodding vigorously.

You chat for a while, as Alexis tells you about her job editing a travel website. She seems very nice, though you notice she has a habit of repeating whatever you say back to you in a slightly different order. Maybe it's an editor thing?

After a while, you come across David sitting on his own.

'Ooh, you're looking thoughtful, Dave,' says Alexis.

'I need to get something off my chest,' says David. 'I've been letting everyone think I run a pub, but I don't. I haven't for a few years now. We had to give it up. And now everyone has been saying they're going to come and visit and asked me what the name of it is and, for some stupid reason, I said it was called the White Lion.'

'Ah, mate,' says Alexis. 'Don't stress about it. Just tell people when it feels right.'

He nods, but is clearly still troubled. At that moment, Gabriel comes through, saying there's talk of a game brewing and would any of you be interested? David shakes his head, but you and Alexis head after Gabriel.

- Turn to **60**.

172

You mull over your choices as you brush your teeth. You think about what you could have done differently, but mostly you're glad you weren't one of the names getting voted for.

Your sleep is uneasy; you keep thinking you can hear footsteps outside the bedroom door. In fact, you're certain of it. Quietly, you inch towards the door. Just as you're reaching for the handle, you're horrified to see it turn. Someone is coming in.

YOU HAVE BEEN MURDERED.

To play this day again, please turn to **110**. Better luck next time!

173

You chip in, admitting that you have heard Tim's name a few times from various people, but as you're speaking, you see the looks on Gabriel's and Gregg's faces and River is gently shaking her head. You do a quick totting-up in your head and you realise that Tim has almost certainly got the votes over Anna. He's made it a straight popularity contest and he's almost certainly going to win. At this stage, you don't want to get caught voting against the room. 'But to be honest with you, I've heard Anna's name mentioned just as often too.'

As the names are revealed, Anna, Ruby and Precious both vote for Tim, restating their original reasoning, but the rest of you vote for Anna. River goes first and says, 'I just didn't hear that passion when you were defending yourself that I'd expect if you were a Faithful.' Everyone else gives some version of that too.

Your Host steps forwards. 'Let's see if you've got it right. Anna, please tell the room, are you Faithful or a Traitor?'

She stands in front of you with a calm smile on her face.

'The numbers never lie. I am a Faithful.'

There is a collective groan. 'I told you,' says Ruby in disgust.

YOU HAVE BANISHED A FAITHFUL.

- Turn to **102**.

174

'It's got to be Ruby, hasn't it?' you say. 'She's like a bloodhound.'

'Well now, we can't go for Ruby,' says Tim. 'Not after she came for me so hard earlier. It'll look like straight revenge. But I do love the idea of breaking up Precious and Ruby. They're becoming a right little unit. Is it too obvious that we're doing that to get to Ruby though?'

You have an idea. 'Could we try and spin that it was exactly what a ruthless Traitor would do?' Both of them nod along. You all decide to murder Precious.

- Turn to **18**.

175

'And he wanted to share it with you privately?' clarifies Gabriel. This makes you feel a bit uneasy, so you explain that you immediately said he should tell it to the whole group at once. You of all people don't want to be standing next to a secret again.

'Oh I'm sure,' says Gabriel. 'Perhaps there's another reason for his secrecy though?' You shrug your shoulders and you both head back downstairs.

- Turn to **134**.

176

'And then there were six,' says your Host. 'You have made it this far. But whose race is run? Tonight you must banish another. Let the games begin.'

River is straight out of the blocks. 'I never normally go first but I really have to tonight. I haven't really felt able to talk to many people today. But I think in a way that might have helped me get perspective on some things. And Tim, you know how much I like and respect you, but after last night, with Anna, it just feels like the room went with our hearts, not our heads.'

Tim is smiling, but he sags a little.

Ruby chips in, 'Well, you all know what I'm going to say, but it's absolutely clear to me who is a Traitor and it's Tim. I tried to show you yesterday but you went with Anna and we banished another Faithful.'

Tim is smiling genially but it looks a bit forced this time. He tries to say that, to his mind, murdering Precious would have been the perfect move for Ruby to make to point the finger away from herself. River is nodding tentatively and Gabriel looks thoughtful too.

You can see that because of Nina, the idea that Tim is a similarly unexpected Traitor still makes a lot of sense to everyone. And where his niceness once seemed like his superpower, suddenly, without it, there are a few examples of people remembering him acting in a way that doesn't quite add up. Gregg chips in with a couple of key examples and now Tim's smile almost entirely falls away under the pressure. Ruby is like a star barrister and keeps him under relentless scrutiny. And like a bad witness, he crumbles. He is hostile and patronising and seems to be flailing around trying to blame everyone. First Gregg, then Ruby, then even River. But nothing lands. It actually really starts to make sense to you.

As the names are revealed, Tim votes for Ruby, but the rest of you vote for Tim.

Your Host steps forwards.

'Let's see if you've got it right. Tim, are you Faithful or a Traitor?' By this time he's regained his composure somewhat.

'Well, everyone, it's truly been a pleasure getting to know every single one of you . . .' Is it you, or does he linger on Gregg and River for longer than anyone else? You think you see something that looks like disappointment.

'But I have to tell you . . . I'm a Traitor.'

Ruby screams and the whole room lets out its breath.

YOU HAVE BANISHED A TRAITOR.

- Turn to **224**.

177

'Welcome,' says your Host when you are all seated. 'For two of you this is your first time at the Round Table. Welcome. The rest of you are veterans. Although yesterday you continued your frankly appalling record of banishing Faithfuls, so I'm not sure how much of an advantage that will be. You have the opportunity to put that right tonight. Have at it!'

'I'm just going to go first, or I'll have stage fright,' says Ruby. 'I think Precious and I are both very aware that we can't really be much use in terms of observations about people. We haven't been here watching like you all have. But I think we might be useful in terms of being more objective.' She takes a sip of water. 'So, I suppose the first question I would ask is has anyone here's behaviour noticeably changed in any way that's not really explainable? I'm not talking about someone being sad or low after a friend was banished or murdered. I mean more fundamental than that.'

Everyone is silent for a moment as they think.

You consider a few options.

What do you do?

- Suggest Tim and his twinkly charm, breezing his way through the day. But has that mask slipped? Turn to **253**.

- Suggest Teddy and his constant game theory, putting himself into the Traitor mindset to try and work out what they think. But has he changed the script? Turn to **309**.

- Suggest Anna and her reliance on numbers and formulae. But has she dropped the ball on that? Turn to **57**.

178

'Wait for me!' you call, and trot after them into the library.

Ruby is running her finger along the shelf of books. 'I wasn't sure if they would be real books,' she says. 'Or that wallpaper that looks like books.' She pulls one off the shelf and opens it.

'You know, it's only in the last couple of years that I've really started reading,' says Tim, settling into an armchair. 'I didn't enjoy school, but now I always have about three books on the go.'

'I'm just going to put this out there with no comment,' says Ruby, 'but I am finding myself more and more interested in how Gregg is behaving.' There is a lot of nodding and Tim taps his nose. Everyone agrees to keep an eye on Gregg.

River is watching them both with a look of genuine affection. You think again how surprising it is that the odds are that one of them is a Traitor. All your time in the Castle so far has made you realise how hard it is to tell if someone is lying.

You all settle into a conversation about your favourite books before you decide you should probably go and see what the others are up to. You don't think you're going to find anything here that helps you ahead of tonight's Round Table, so you make your excuses and head out.

- Turn to **250**.

179

Quite right! The minimum number with two people in armour is 9. First, two unarmoured people cross, then one rows back and waves off an armoured person by themselves. Then the unarmoured person who had remained crosses, takes the other unarmoured person to the other side and returns alone to get the boat where we want it. An armoured person can then cross, and we repeat until everyone is home and dry. Return to **96** to continue.

MISSION

THE SAUCY CHINS

In the dining hall, you're split into groups of two, three and four – and served pizza. The slices are very, very sloppy and the fancy napkins you've become used to seeing on the table (the thickness of which is actually a source of great pleasure for you) are absent today.

You will soon find out why.

Screens are brought in and now each group of two, three or four can only see each other. (You're in a three, with Nina and Gabriel.) You are all told that if you see anyone else with pizza sauce on their chin, you will be unable to help yourself from sniggering.

Sure enough, the air in the dining hall is soon filled with sniggers: some surreptitious, some a little too loud, to be honest.

After a few moments, a gong sounds and silence is

restored. You are all asked if there were any groups in which no one was sniggering. There were not. Everyone is asked whether they can tell whether their own chin has got pizza sauce on it. The people in pairs say that they can, but nobody else does. (Not even Teddy or any of the other people who are averse to admitting there's something they don't know.)

A pause. (A significant pause, in more ways than one.) You are now asked: in which, if any, of the groups, could you know for sure whether you yourself had pizza sauce on your chin?

Your answer is that you would know you had a saucy chin if you were . . .

- *. . . in any of the groups*. Turn to **98**.

- *. . . only in the groups of two and three*. Turn to **275**.

- *. . . only in the groups of two*. Turn to **161**.

- *. . . in none of the groups*. Turn to **170**.

- When you are finished, turn to **21**.

181

You keep listening, but you soon realise that you're not actually paying attention to anything she's saying. Instead, you're noticing who's coming in and who isn't. Isla is craning her neck to see who's here, presumably checking for Amrit, you think. Most people look apprehensive. Rakayah doesn't, but then she seems generally pretty unflappable. And once Teddy and Gregg appear (at the same time) and your Host nods to indicate that everyone who's survived is here, you realise who hasn't.

- Turn to **155**.

182

After the Mission, everyone is energised, and any divide earlier in the day feels long forgotten.

You go into the corridor, smiling at how competitive everyone has become.

You pass Elif, Alexis and David, who seem to be having a conversation about their pets. 'With dogs,' says David, 'you get the feeling that they would run into a burning building to save you. With cats, it's more that they might start the fire because they're interested to see what might happen.'

Amrit and Isla pass in the other direction, giggling about something.

It turns out Jorge and Rakayah like some of the same music, though Jorge can't believe it when Rakayah says she's really into 'classics'.

'Classics!' he roars. 'My god, that makes me feel old.'

You are happy to just watch and listen to the conversations around you. But all too soon you are told it's time for Round Table.

- Turn to **165**.

183

You sit quietly and into the gap Ruby speaks eloquently and passionately about why she is Faithful. But she also lets River have it for trying to guide the room again, which she says is a big red flag for her.

You nod vigorously, and Gabriel is looking at both of you a little strangely. Perhaps this confrontation has been too much for someone as finely tuned to pleasantry as him.

All too soon, it's time. But this time you are collected and taken down to the front of the Castle. In the shadows you think you must be where you had first stood on the grass what seems like a lifetime ago. Your Host steps forwards.

- Turn to **94**.

184

'I really wasn't expecting it to all be this hard. The thought of murders and banishments, of Traitors walking amongst us.' You glance down at the table, your voice catching. 'It's just a lot, isn't it?'

Tim nods his head and Anna, who is next to him, pats your hand.

You notice a couple of people looking at you and nodding in sympathy. But you wonder if you see Steve-O roll their eyes.

Who is missing?! As you begin to tick off who isn't there yet, you realise that there are two people missing: Luke and Elif. There is a knock on the door and then an expectant hush. Elif comes into the room, smiling nervously. She is mobbed by curious people and says, 'I don't know, I just don't know – all I know is that I'm a Faithful.'

'Oh no, Luke,' says Nina, sadly. And you realise that some people have already begun to form strong attachments. You're going to need to up your game.

At that moment, your Host enters.

'Good morning everyone. I hope you all slept well. Unfortunately, there was no rest for the wicked. As you will no doubt have worked out, last night Luke was murdered by the Traitors.'

- Turn to **36**.

185

Reasoning that your only hope in this game is to be a leader not a follower, you stride confidently over to stand on the furthest green section on the floor. Next to you is Precious (Skye, 28), who gives you an encouraging smile. 'No point in being mealy-mouthed, is there? Hiding your light under a bushel.' Trying to soften things a little, in case someone is listening, you say, 'I really have no idea but I certainly *hope* I'll give it my best shot!' There's shuffling next to you as people swap position at the last moment.

'Now please stop moving!' The Host peers over at you. 'We asked you to make a decision. And told you that every decision has con-sequences. Well, here you are. This is a game where pride always comes before a fall.' She gestures to you and Precious. 'So I'm afraid, both of you are going home.'

At first people smile, and you think perhaps it's a joke. But there is no smile on your Host's face. You can't believe it – your adventure is over before it even began. As people hug you goodbye and turn to go inside the Castle, and the cars arrive to take you and Precious away, you curse your decision to not be true to yourself.

YOU HAVE LEFT THE GAME.

Please return to **1**. Better luck next time!

186

In the library it's cool and quiet. You sink into one of the armchairs when you're startled by a voice close by.

'Are you hiding too?' asks River. You can't help but jump. 'Don't panic,' she says quietly. 'Just act exactly as you would have done yesterday.'

'I can't get over how hard this is.'

'You're doing well. Now, quick, I feel like I have no idea what's going to happen tonight because I've been keeping a low profile,' she says. 'I've ducked out of pretty much every chance to talk to anyone. At the risk of making you do my homework, what's every-one talking about? How's the heat on Tim after last night?'

You think for a moment. It has felt as if the main gossip you've heard has been about her and Tim. Here is an opportunity to give a heads-up to Team Traitor. Or to muddy the waters. After all, if the group are thrown another Traitor tonight, they'll be less likely to turn their attention to you, won't they?

What do you do?

- Tell River that people are considering both her and Tim. Turn to **137**.

- Keep quiet about what you've heard. Turn to **234**.

187

You're relieved that you weren't as loud as you thought you were going to be, as you disguise your laugh as a cough, then return what feels like a friendly, innocent gaze back at Teddy (he does have quite a penetrating stare, you notice) and he carries on until he seems to have assessed everyone.

'Interesting,' is all he says at first.

'There are two people who I think couldn't look me in the eye. Tim and Steve-O. I reckon at least one of them is very likely a Traitor.'

Steve-O is the first to pipe up. 'What? This is mad. I mean, we could all have said we can "read people" and done what Teddy did, and then we'd have different names to be talking about.' He's quite agitated, especially in comparison to Tim, who's just smiling benignly. 'We should forget what just happened and try and think about something we all agree on, not some random's gut!'

Ooh. Calling Teddy 'some random' sounded bad. Steve-O knows it and tries to backpedal. 'I mean, you're not some random, but come on. Guys?'

Irwin, though, acts like the task now is to choose between Steve-O and Tim. 'What about you, Tim?'

Tim's still just smiling, a picture of calm. 'I suppose,' he says at last, 'I did have something to hide when you were gazing at me, Teddy.'

'See?' barks Teddy. 'I can always tell.'

'But goodness me, it's not that I'm a Traitor. I just, well, I was thinking a couple of things. That this is a silly way to choose who we might banish – I do apologise, Teddy, but it is what I think – and I was also thinking, "Oh dear, I bet I'm going to do something to draw attention to myself." And I'm rather afraid I did!'

'OK, thanks Tim,' says Irwin. 'You know, it's a tough decision, this one. I do like you both, and—'

'Hang on,' says Steve-O. 'I mean, why are we rushing? You could just as well say a Traitor would have a good reason for wanting the vote to be between me and Tim. Yeah? Like you're doing, Irwin.'

'Hey, I'm happy to be in the mix if you want,' says Irwin.

You think you know what he's doing. He's figured that Steve-O is likely to go, and thinks that if he's nominated now as well, he's probably safe for a bit. 'In fact, let's also vote on whether to choose from me, Steve-O and Tim, or to carry on.'

Judging by the murmuring, this seems to be generally thought to be fair.

'OK then,' says Irwin. 'Shall we go to the vote, or talk it out a bit more? Raise your hand if you want to move on and vote.'

The easy thing to do would be to raise your hand and get on with things while the going is good. Why talk yourself into trouble? However, if your suspicions about Steve-O's race being run are correct, why not use the opportunity to build up a bit of personal credit and show you're a leader?

What do you do?

- Vote to go straight to the vote. Turn to **296**.

- Vote to talk it out a bit more. Turn to **52**.

188

As you all begin to get up and leave the room, Deb takes you by the arm. 'Fancy coming for a natter?' she asks conspiratorially.

Deb is very nice and everyone likes her, so it wouldn't be the worst idea in the world to put a bit of time into establishing bonds with her. On the other hand, you're pretty sure that she'd always be swayed by the last person she spoke to, or a butterfly or something shiny – then feel immediately very mean.

What do you do?

- Go out with Deb to the steps by the pillars, where a number of the younger ones have taken to sunning them-selves. Turn to **286**.

- Politely decline Deb, walk out into the grounds and leave your options open. Turn to **116**.

'Hey, room for a little one?' you call out. Gabriel, Anna and Nina slow down and you all step out into the already bright sunshine.

'Walk or chairs?' says Nina. You try to work out if there's a better answer to give but then catch yourself and you're just honest.

'Today feels like a lazy day,' you say. Everyone agrees and you all sit down.

'I'm just going to say it because I think we're all thinking it,' says Nina, 'but would even this place be twisted enough to send one or both of Precious and Ruby in as a Traitor?' You admit that you've been thinking that too and come to the conclusion that you can't rule anything out.

'The real problem is,' says Anna, 'we have nothing to benchmark their behaviours against.'

'Well,' says Gabriel, 'I feel pretty confident that Ruby isn't a Traitor. That question she asked last night pretty much directly led to Teddy's demise. So unless Traitors have started knocking each other off, that feels like a strong clue to me. Precious, I feel like I haven't met her enough to make my mind up.' Everyone nods along at that.

The conversation moves on to nostalgia around childhood summers gone by, which were always sunny and seemed to last forever. You're getting too hot and want to at least check in with the others, so you say goodbye and head inside.

- Turn to **303**.

Trying to hold in any potential laughter, you squirm a little as Teddy eyes you up and down. You don't think anyone can really have noticed, but you're still glad when he moves on to the next person.

Finally, he taps his fingers together. At first, all he says is: 'Interesting.'

And then, after another pause: 'I'm gonna name two people who I didn't think were giving me honest vibes . . .' And to your horror, the names are Tim's and yours.

'What!?' you bark.

'And possibly Steve-O,' adds Teddy.

'Hang on a mo, you said you were picking two,' protests Steve-O.

Tim doesn't seem to be saying much; in fact, he's smiling. Everything seems to be moving much too quickly for your comfort.

'But you're not saying you *know*,' you offer to Teddy. You can hear that your voice sounds desperate, but you have to say something. 'Right, Teddy? It was just a moment?'

'What can I tell you? I have to call it like I see it,' says Teddy.

'And we have to eliminate someone,' chimes in Irwin. 'I'd hate to see either of you go, but this is what we're doing.'

You have one moment to try and swing things your way.

What do you do?

- Attack Steve-O's character and try and drag him into it. Turn to **42**.

- Be honest as to why you weren't able to meet Teddy's eye and appeal to people's good natures. Turn to **10**.

191

As you trudge into the now familiar room, you feel sure it will feature in your dreams in the future. The dynamic has changed now there are fewer people. It feels more intimate and personal somehow. Everyone seems to know everyone's business in a way they couldn't when there were more people and they naturally broke up into smaller groups.

'Well, I'm happy to go first this time,' says Nina. But Jorge leans forwards.

'I'm very sorry, Nina, but I have to ask you something first.' Nina looks shocked at the interruption but waves her hand in invitation for him to speak.

'It's been brought to my attention that Deb was overheard calling you "Gran" earlier today. I have to ask. Are you related?'

Nina looks crestfallen. 'That's actually what I was about to say. Yes, Deb is my granddaughter.' There is a gasp in the room. 'I have wanted to tell you all so many times, but at first I didn't know people well enough, and then, well, winning would change

Deb's life. And she deserves only good things. Living in different countries, I haven't always been able to be there for birthdays and Christmas. And she's such a good girl.' Her voice catches and she waves her hand in apology.

'I felt so guilty about being wrong about Isla. I thought you'd all hate me if you knew I was keeping this secret too.' Both Nina and Deb stare down at the table in shame.

There is silence for a moment, then Gregg says grumpily, 'Who told you, Jorge?'

Your heart starts to beat. You have to act quickly. Do you volunteer the information, or let Jorge do it?

What do you do?

- Speak up. Turn to **235**.

- Keep quiet. Turn to **209**.

BONUS GAME

CAPTURE THE CASTLE: DISRUPTOR

You need: deck of cards, phone with timer

Players: Town Crier, plus at least two others

Take from the deck two 2s (the Renegades) and one 7 (the Disruptor). Then add court cards (king, queen, jack) until there are three more cards than there are players.

One player is the Town Crier and should now read the text below.

I am shuffling the cards, and dealing one to everyone, including myself.

I am now placing the remaining cards face down in a row on the table.

Everyone, look at your card. If you have a 2, you are a Renegade, come to capture the castle. If you have a 7, you are the Disruptor. Everyone else is a member of the Royal Family.

Place your card face down, close to the three already on the table in a way that makes it clear whose is whose.

When I say, 'Let us dance!', the Masked Ball will commence. Everyone – including me – will close their eyes for a count of eight. During that time, any Renegades must open their eyes and clock each other.

Ready . . . Let us dance! One, two, three, four, five, six, seven . . . eight.

Everyone must open their eyes. The King has heard that there may be a Renegade at his Masked Ball. In five minutes' time, he will have someone thrown in the stocks. You have five minutes to debate whom to put in the stocks. Any of you may claim to have been assigned any of the identities: Royal Family, Renegade or Disruptor.

During the debate, any player may declare themselves to be the Disruptor. If this happens, all players will pass their card to the person on their left and will have the identity of their new card. If multiple players claim to be the Disruptor, the cards will move multiple times.

The time starts . . . now.

Set the timer, and then when the time is up . . .

After a count of five, we shall all vote. The player or players with the most votes shall be placed in the stocks.

If one or more Renegades is placed in the stocks, the Royal Family shall be declared victorious. If there were no Renegades, the Royal Family shall be declared victorious. In all other situations, the Renegades shall be declared victorious. If you decide that the King should exhibit *clemency, you should now agree to each vote for the player on your left, and nobody shall be placed in the stocks.*

I shall now make the count of five. One, two, three, four, five.

NB: this game can be combined with other Capture the Castle games in the list of games at the start of the book, so long as the total number of cards is always topped up to three more than the number of players using members of the Royal Family.

- Turn to **70**.

Hoping you have interpreted River's facial expression correctly, you write Gabriel. Ruby writes River. River has written your name. (So much for loyalty). Gabriel has written your name.

You step forwards. And your Host asks you to say if you are Faithful or a Traitor.

'I'm so happy to have made it to the end. I've learnt so much here and met such amazing people. That's why I'm happy you worked out I'm a Traitor.' Ruby whoops as you are led away.

YOU HAVE BEEN BANISHED.

To play this day again, please turn to **267**. Better luck next time!

You leave the room and go to join the others, who are waiting to enter the Round Table, a dark, wood-panelled room with a large circular table in its centre. It can only be your imagination but you think that people are looking at you differently as you all file in and sit down. Elif clutches her notebook tightly as she stares across the table in your direction. What will she write about you? 'Quite obviously Traitor material'? Stop it, you tell yourself, you're getting carried away.

But could it be true that your capacity to be a Traitor is showing on your face already? You suddenly become very aware of your hands as you sit down, folding them on the table, then on your lap. You worry that everyone else in the room can hear your heart beating.

- Turn to **257**.

195

'Well, it felt like the room got close with Tim last night,' you say. 'Then he made his switch and they went to Anna. I'm not saying I'm totally agreeing with you. But I'm not ruling it out either.'

'Ooh, careful with those splinters in your bum from sitting on that fence!' says Ruby. You can't help but warm to her. She's forthright and charming. All the qualities you'd need to be a brilliant Traitor, you immediately think.

'Let's both just keep a very beady eye on Tim,' she says. And you nod.

'Right. We should go join up with the others,' Ruby says. 'Before they start to gossip!'

As you head back inside you are just in time to meet everyone gathering in the breakfast room.

'We don't have many more of these together,' says your Host. 'So let's make sure today is a great Mission.'

- Turn to **252**.

196

Having been burnt a couple of times by being too visible, you decide to keep this to yourself. You like Deb and Nina and don't want to spread rumours about them. Plus, perhaps it makes more sense to keep your powder dry for Round Table. No sense in giving up a move too early. The conversation moves on to which of those in the Castle will stay in touch afterwards, and you nod and smile, letting the babble of voices wash over you.

The rest of the day passes without incident until it's time for Round Table.

- Turn to **54**.

197

'Hey, wait for me,' you call. Gabriel turns, looking startled. Then smiles when he sees you. 'I was just going to collect my thoughts before the day kicks off, but I know you won't throw lots of theories at me, so you can join me.'

You both sit in companiable silence for a while.

'I have basically no idea who is a Traitor,' says Gabriel finally. 'Apart from that I know I'm not, and I'm pretty sure you're not. But the other three, I have no idea. When I'm with them, I think they're definitely not, and then realise that's exactly what a good Traitor would make you think. Whatever happens, someone we've trusted has been lying to us. So who knows!'

You are glad that Gabriel has his eyes closed, or you feel sure he'd notice your face burning red with a surprising amount of shame. Even though you remind yourself that you haven't been lying the entire time, it feels like you're lying to people you now consider friends.

You chat for a bit about how everyone responded to the revelation that Tim was a Traitor. You are aware of wanting to not be overly protective of River and you suggest that Gregg would have taken his mentor figure lying to him hard. You make a mental note to try and flag this to River.

'Well, I'll leave you to it,' you say, and Gabriel salutes goodbye.

- Turn to **310**.

198

'Well, I don't think you're one, and I know I'm not!' announces Alexis airily when you're on your own. You both laugh. 'What did you think to Teddy's theory? I kind of thought you looked like you might agree?'

'Oh, very much so,' you say. 'I think we need to start getting into the heads of the Traitors more.'

Alexis is nodding vigorously. 'I totally agree. There's no way the Traitors would be stupid enough to bump someone off who was threatened by them so directly like that.'

You chat for a while, as Alexis tells you about her job editing a travel website. She seems very nice, though you notice she has a habit of repeating whatever you say back to you in a slightly different order. Maybe it's an editor thing?

After a while, you come across David sitting on his own.

'Ooh, you're looking thoughtful, Dave,' says Alexis.

'I need to get something off my chest,' says David. 'I've been letting everyone think I run a pub, but I don't. I haven't for a few years now. We had to give it up. And now everyone has been saying they're going to come and visit and asked me what the name of it is and, for some stupid reason, I said it was called the White Lion.'

'Ah, mate,' says Alexis. 'Don't stress about it. Just tell people when it feels right.'

He nods, but is clearly still troubled. At that moment, Gabriel comes through, saying there's talk of a game brewing and would any of you be interested? David shakes his head, but you and Alexis head after Gabriel.

- Turn to **60**.

199

You have wasted a lot of time, and that's kind of a big deal when some of the rowers are wearing heavy chainmail. Return to **96** and try again.

Everyone compares notes on who they've noticed spending lots of time together. You join in, but quietly, happy to listen to what everyone else has to say. At one point, Anna, who you hadn't noticed standing by the window, says that we need to be paying attention to people, not numbers and everyone nods along vaguely.

'You're awfully quiet there,' says River, holding her coffee mug in both hands and looking at you. You feel everyone's eyes on you. 'Do you think the Traitors are likely to have paired off?'

Mindful of your choice to play things safe for a bit longer, you just smile and sip your coffee.

'Honestly,' you say, 'I'm finding it hard enough to remember everyone's name. Never mind coming up with a grand theory for anything!' People laugh, and River smiles but is still looking at you with a fixed expression. 'I wish I'd brought a little book like Elif did,' you say.

'But you forgot,' says Tim, and everyone laughs.

- Turn to **72**.

'It's absolutely fascinating, isn't it?' you say. 'Like a psychological experiment or something.'

Anna nods with a slightly puzzled look on her face. To the other side of you, River is watching you intently with a kind of shocked fascination and you realise you might have gone too far.

Who is missing?! As you begin to tick off who isn't there yet, you realise that two people are missing: Luke and Elif. There is a knock on the door and then an expectant hush. Elif comes into the room, smiling nervously. She is mobbed by curious people and says, 'I don't know, I just don't know – all I know is that I'm a Faithful.'

'Oh no, Luke,' says Nina, sadly. And you realise that some people have already begun to form strong attachments. You're going to need to up your game.

At that moment, your Host enters.

'Good morning everyone. I hope you all slept well. Unfortunately, there was no rest for the wicked. As you will no doubt have worked out, last night Luke was murdered by the Traitors.'

- Turn to **36**.

202

DAY 3

The mood is sombre as you enter the breakfast room this morning. The banishment process last night was clearly difficult for everyone. There are only a few of you when you first enter to – you are gratified to hear – a handful of people cheering.

You sit between Rakayah and Gregg. Rakayah is dabbing sporadically at her eyes with a napkin. 'I think it's because I'm very empathetic,' she says. 'I feel things very deeply.'

Gregg is getting stuck into a pile of scrambled eggs. 'Well, they certainly got their money's worth out of us last night, didn't they? What drama!'

People file in, one by one, until it becomes clear that only David and Irwin are missing. Interesting.

There is a knock on the door. Everyone pauses . . . as David walks in, smiling broadly. People cheer but then there's silence.

Jorge is the first to say it. 'Irwin has been murdered!' Rakayah only half muffles a strangled cry.

'I don't believe it,' says Amrit. 'I just don't believe it, man.'

But it's real. Conversation, of course, turns to speculation about motive. Gabriel says the most 'salient' thing about Irwin was his having pushed for acting on Teddy's instinct last night.

'Riiiiight,' replies Gregg, 'so you gotta ask who benefited from that and who was threatened. And I'm not being funny, Tim, but it looked like it was going to get hairy for you for a moment back there.'

You consider this as the conversation develops. Some people have moved on, including a still bleary-eyed Rakayah. For you, this makes sense on the face of it, but you figure that if you were a Traitor, in Tim's position, the last thing you would do is draw attention to yourself in that way. Yesterday, you let others lead the conversation and it got pretty uncomfortable. Is it time for the boot to be on the other foot?

What do you do?

- Voice your thoughts. Turn to **263**.

- Keep them to yourself. Turn to **121**.

203

After another five minutes of holding forth, you deliver your final bon mot to appreciative smiles. 'Blimey, I felt like I was in the audience of a TedTalk for a minute there,' says Irwin.

You wave your hand modestly. 'Hardly. I'm just muddling through.'

The gong sounds and you all catch each other's eye. Bed time.

- Turn to **226**.

MISSION

DOUBLE AMNESIA

You need: sticky notes and pencils

Each player chooses two identities for the person on their left.

Each identity can be someone you know, a fictional person, a famous person, someone from history . . . but the more villainous the better.

Write the names clearly on two sticky notes and give them to the person on your left.

They must, without reading the notes, attach them to their forehead so that everyone can see.

The oldest player starts. Like all the players, she or he has Double Amnesia and must try to 'recall' both of their identities by asking the room a yes/no question to help guess the name on the notes.

They will not know which of the names the answer refers to.

If the answer is 'yes', the player can ask another question. If it's 'no' (or 'maybe', 'sort of', etcetera), play passes to the left.

At any point, the question can be 'Am I . . . ?', completed with a guess as to a name. If the guess is correct, the player should be told which sticky note to remove.

Once a player has guessed both identities (recovered from Double Amnesia), they leave the game but can still answer questions.

The last player to recover from Double Amnesia is the loser.

Variant: *Try warming up with just one name assigned to each player.*

After the Mission, the winning team trot off happily to the Armoury; although you tried your hardest, your team weren't successful. You make a note of River's aptitude both for noticing who has contributed to a success and for telling those people what they did right. She can even find something encouraging to say about someone who's been close to dead weight. It's a skill.

Then, everyone disperses into smaller groups scattered around the Castle. You watch Precious and Gregg wandering away, but they both seem deep in thought, so you leave them to it.

River, Tim and Ruby head for the library. Gabriel, Anna and Nina head for the steps.

What do you do?

- Go with River, Tim and Ruby. Turn to **178**.

- Go with Gabriel, Anna and Nina. Turn to **189**.

205

Anna says thank you, also a little imperiously to your mind, and says that irrespective of which players happen to be the Traitors, she has calculated that today is mathematically more likely to produce a successful banishment.

'The numbers are complex,' she adds, 'but risk management sometimes gives the same results as instinct. And though we can't forget that there are those among us deliberately adding bad information by lying, they can't keep their presence hidden. We just need to think who we've seen nudging conversations along.'

OK, you say to yourself. This is the most important moment for you so far. You feel you've made some unwise decisions in the past, so . . . now is the time to learn from them. And the very act of entertaining this thought – of concentrating on a solution rather than dwelling on a problem – makes you happier. You can feel it, physically. You relax your shoulders and gaze around the table as if you haven't a care in the world.

Gabriel points out that Deb has seemed on edge today. For herself, Deb reiterates that she holds her hands up to having messed up yesterday. 'And any of you would feel the same.' There's a pause and it feels like your moment. But what should you say? You know you need to own the narrative.

What Anna said about people nudging conversations has made you think of something, but you don't know what.

What do you do?

- Head off the attack from Gregg you are sure is about to come. Turn to **166**.

- Draw attention to Rakayah's behaviour. Turn to **152**.

206

'Well, it's that time again,' says the Host. 'Yesterday, you banished a Faithful. Will you make the same mistake again? Or will you snare a Traitor? Whatever happens, one more of you must leave.'

Looking around the table, it seems as if everyone has their game face on. Yesterday, there was a kind of lightness, as no one quite knew what to expect. You feel calm.

'I'll go first this time,' says Jorge, smiling. 'I know we've all been having various conversations. And it's been very interesting to see who has been leading conversations and who has been following them. I just want to throw out the name of someone who I feel has been very actively convincing people to see things a certain way. And that's you, Alexis.'

You see the look of shock on her face. As others start to chime in, they refer to Alexis's theory.

She looks across at you pleadingly. Could you help her?

What do you do?

- Come to Alexis's aid. Turn to **80**.

- Let her flounder. You don't want to be dragged down with her. Turn to **268**.

207

'Yes, we should definitely be thinking about people who are spending time together,' you say. 'It may well be that, if you're a Traitor, you want to spend time with people who appreciate what you're going through.' You pause and everyone is engaged, looking at you. 'But equally, maybe they're wise to that idea, so maybe they are doing exactly the opposite. Staying away from each other and making sure they're spreading their time between everyone pretty equally.'

'Exactly,' says Anna, who you hadn't noticed standing by the window. 'It's like my job, we need to pay attention to people, not numbers.' River looks at you, nodding vigorously. Are you imagining it, or does Rakayah have a newfound look of admiration on her face?

The coffee is strong, and you start to feel properly awake for the first time that morning. People are comparing notes, doing exactly what you had suggested. It feels good to have your ideas listened to.

You make your excuses and head out into the corridor.

- Turn to **72**.

The mood is celebratory as you all toast your success. Precious and Ruby are feted as good luck charms. There is all sorts of chat about how many Traitors there are left.

But no one dwells for too long on this detail. The sound of laughter is still echoing in your head as it hits the pillow. If you go tonight, at least you'll go happy.

- Turn to **258**.

You try to look back out at the room steadily, but when Jorge tells them it was you, you can't help but flinch. And that's all the invitation Deb needs to start speaking first.

'I'm sorry, I know we told a lie and that's bad.' She looks at you. 'But this is about the fourth time now you've been at the centre of things, whispering in people's ears. We've all realised that the Traitors are manipulating us, guiding us – well, that's one hundred per cent you. I can hand on my heart say that this lie didn't benefit me and that I'm a Faithful, but I just don't think you can say the same.'

Even Nina manages to rally: 'I thought we were good enough friends that you would come and talk to me about this, but the fact that you didn't and told tales behind my back is really hurtful.'

And that seems to be the final nail in the coffin. The room's sense of hurt feelings about being told a lie for so long seems to be transformed into anger at you. Suddenly everyone is remembering times that you've been there skulking in the shadows.

You don't really need to look at the names as they come up to know that yours will be written the most. As you stand to tell them they have made a mistake, you wonder if they will even care. There was something primal at work there. They needed a scapegoat and it was you.

YOU HAVE BEEN BANISHED.

To play this day again, please turn to **245**. Better luck next time!

210

'Now,' says your Host. 'This is where things get really serious. If you are absolutely confident that all of you are Faithfuls, then we can stop the game now. But remember, if there is a Traitor here, then they have won. So, if you wish, you can make the decision to banish one further person. Which will you choose?' Your Host gestures for you to look next to you. 'Beside you is a chest with two ceremonial pouches in it. One is labelled "End Game". The other "Banish Again". When you have made your decision, hand over your chosen pouch and we will reveal your decision. If any one of you chooses to banish again, you all must.'

Your head is spinning. In the whirl of elation at making it through to this stage, you hadn't even thought that this might not be the end. But of course there is one final twist. You look around you. Ruby is frowning and looking at River. Gabriel looks serene. There is something about what happened when Tim left that you still can't get out of your head. Like an itch you just can't scratch.

At the last moment, you grab the 'Banish Again' pouch and hand it over.

'First, River,' says your Host. The pouch is thrown into the fire and green smoke rises. *End Game.*

'Now, Gabriel,' says your Host. Another pouch and green smoke, curling up into the night sky, lit by the flames. *End Game.*

When your pouch goes into the fire, the smoke is red, swirling around you. *Banish Again.*

'Now, Ruby,' says your Host. Appropriately, the smoke is lit ruby. *Banish Again.*

'So,' your Host says, 'you're not sure. Time to take your slates and write the name of who you will now banish.'

What do you do?

- Write Gabriel. Turn to **281**.

- Write River. Turn to **306**.

- Write Ruby. Turn to **153**.

'Eight of you remain,' says your Host as you sit at the Round Table, your heart beating so loudly you wonder if people can hear it. You think you've made it through the day without making any blunders. But really, who knows. 'We are well past the end of the beginning and may even be approaching the beginning of the end. So once more, it's time to decide. Who will you banish?'

As soon as the Host has stopped talking, Ruby jumps in.

'OK, I can't not start tonight. Gregg.' She turns to face him directly and he nods at her. 'I can't be the only one who's noticed that you seem to be sad about banishing a Traitor and that's weird.' Anna joins in. 'It's, what we call in the trade, an anomaly.' Ruby starts straight back in. 'But I can't make up my mind whether you're just *that* sensitive, or you feel guilty about banishing a fellow Traitor. But I actually want to leave that to the side for now. Tim.'

Tim makes a little fake jump. 'Present,' he says, laughing. But Ruby doesn't smile back.

'I hear you think I'm a Traitor.' She is smiling at him but it's not a friendly smile.

'I don't think I've actually ever said that,' says Tim. 'I've just been saying we need to consider everyone.'

'I agree,' says Ruby. 'So let's consider you. And Anna and her vending machines.'

'Let's just take a bit of a breath,' says River. 'I know we were all shocked by Nina but that doesn't mean we have to suddenly all do 180-degree turns and start saying everyone is a . . . vending machine.'

Ruby and Precious both talk about how often Tim and Anna are at the edge of situations nudging things. Gregg, clearly sensing an opportunity to get the heat off of him chips in. 'You know what, Ruby,' he says, 'I've actually been thinking exactly the same thing today. Being away from the group a bit has made me realise how we've never actually considered Anna. Perhaps we should?'

Anna tries to take the conversation back to Gregg's behaviour and Gregg is looking increasingly nervous. But Tim says, 'For what it's worth, I genuinely think that Gregg is just that nice a bloke. That might not mean much coming from me for some people, but I have to speak the truth.'

Gregg looks at Tim so purely grateful and in such a genuine way, you notice the whole room clock it. 'Yes,' says Anna, clearly frustrated. 'But you must all see that the most logical solution is that Tim and Gregg are both Traitors. Surely?!'

'I don't know about logic,' says Tim. 'Ask me about litter bins and the like and I'll be more help. All I know is that this world is split into two types of people: those who walk on the grass, even though there's a sign. And those that don't. And I'm bloody sure I don't walk on the grass and I don't reckon my mate Gregg does either. I leave it up to you to judge but I won't blame any of you whatever you decide.' You feel like applauding. It's a great speech, and you realise that River must have found a way of giving him the heads-up. Which also means she's unlikely to be voting against him tonight.

Ruby was rolling her eyes the entire time at Precious, but you can tell the room is turning. Gabriel just sits in silence; it's as if he's a kid and his parents are arguing.

Anna senses the mood and tries to win the room, but she just keeps appealing to logic. At one point she tries to make a joke about percentages that falls entirely flat. She finishes speaking with no one looking that convinced.

There's a pause and you realise this would be the time to nudge things. But how subtle should you be? Go all out in defence of Tim, or be more subtle?

What do you do?

- Be even-handed. Turn to **85**.

- Defend Tim and go after Anna. Turn to **249**.

212

As it's a beautiful morning, you all wander together down towards the lake and sit on the grass, watching the ducks bob their heads under the water.

'This is all probably a bit coals to Newcastle for you, Tim, isn't it?' says Nina.

'Oh God, no,' says Tim. 'These ducks make mine look like Dickensian orphans. These have all their own feathers and everything.'

Gregg and Precious are deep in conversation and for a brief and very mean moment you remark to yourself that he doesn't seem to be pining for Deb any more. But you obviously can't share the thought.

Anna shows everyone how to make a daisy necklace, and Gregg kneels down on one knee to present his to Precious, and she pretends to be overcome with emotion, like she's just been proposed to.

River puts hers on her head as a flower crown and does a hippy dance. 'Bellis perennis, the common daisy,' says Nina. 'Gorgeous.'

You lie back on the grass and look up at the sky above you. Just a single cloud in the whole endless expanse of pale blue. You must have dozed because you are woken with the news that it's time for the day's Mission.

- Turn to **204**.

213

'Oh, I don't know about any of that.' You keep your face studiously blank.

River is nodding along. 'Oh sure, I have no real strong sense. But Gregg's certainly had a lot of things that have distracted anyone from looking at him, hasn't he?'

Ruby comes out and says, 'Last game in the library before tonight?' And you both head back inside.

- Turn to **288**.

'Eight of you remain,' says your Host as you sit at the Round Table. 'We are well past the end of the beginning and may even be approaching the beginning of the end. So once more, it's time to decide. Who will you banish?'

As soon as the Host has stopped talking, Ruby jumps in.

'OK, I can't not start tonight. Gregg.' She turns to face him directly and he nods at her. 'I can't be the only one who's noticed that you seem to be sad about banishing a Traitor and that's weird.' Anna joins in. 'It's, what we call in the trade, an anomaly.' Ruby starts straight back in. 'But I can't make up my mind whether you're just *that* sensitive, or you feel guilty about banishing a fellow Traitor. But I actually want to leave that to the side for now. Tim.'

Tim makes a little fake jump. 'Present,' he says, laughing. But Ruby doesn't smile back.

'I hear you think I'm a Traitor.' She is smiling at him but it's not a friendly smile.

'I don't think I've actually ever said that,' says Tim. 'I've just been saying we need to consider everyone.'

'I agree,' says Ruby. 'So let's consider you. And Anna and her vending machines.'

'Let's just take a bit of a breath,' says River. 'I know we were all shocked by Nina but that doesn't mean we have to suddenly all do 180-degree turns and start saying everyone is a . . . vending machine.'

Ruby and Precious both talk about how often Tim and Anna are at the edge of situations, nudging things. Gregg, clearly sensing an opportunity to get the heat off him, chips in. 'You know what, Ruby,' he says, 'I've actually been thinking exactly the same thing today. Being away from the group a bit has made me realise how we've never actually considered Anna. Perhaps we should?'

Anna tries to take the conversation back to Gregg's behaviour and Gregg is looking increasingly nervous. But Tim says, 'For what it's worth, I genuinely think that Gregg is just that nice a bloke. That might not mean much coming from me for some people, but I have to speak the truth.'

Gregg looks at Tim so purely grateful and in such a genuine way, you notice the whole room clock it. 'Yes,' says Anna, clearly frustrated. 'But you must all see that the most logical solution is that Tim and Gregg are both Traitors. Surely?!'

'I don't know about logic,' says Tim. 'Ask me about litter bins and the like and I'll be more help. All I know is that this world is split into two types of people: those who walk on the grass, even though there's a sign. And those that don't. And I'm bloody sure I don't walk on the grass and I don't reckon my mate Gregg does either. I leave it up to you to judge but I won't blame any of you whatever you decide.' Ruby is clearly rolling her eyes but you can tell the room is turning. Gabriel just sits in silence; it's as if he's a kid and his parents are arguing.

Anna senses the mood and tries to win the room, but she just keeps appealing to logic. At one point she tries to make a joke about percentages that falls entirely flat. She finishes speaking, with no one looking that convinced.

There's a pause.

What do you do?

- Encourage the scrutiny of Tim. Turn to **173**.

- Defend Tim and go after Anna. Turn to **109**.

215

After a last-minute change of heart based on nothing more than the facial expression she pulls as you're looking at everyone, you write Ruby. Ruby writes River. River has written your name. Gabriel has written River.

'River, you have been banished. Please tell us if you are Faithful or a Traitor.'

She steps forwards. 'This has been one of the most incredible experiences of my life. I'm proud to have made it this far. And I'm proud of you all. Because I am a Traitor.' Ruby can't help but yelp as River is led quietly away. The three of you who remain look at each other, smiling. Surely there can't be one final twist. Can there?!

'So,' says your Host. 'The final three. Please step forwards and reveal whether you are Faithful or a Traitor.'

Gabriel steps forwards, smiling. 'When I came in here, I knew I just wanted to be me, whatever else happened. I wanted to be true to myself. And that's why I'm so happy to say that I am a Faithful.'

You step forwards solemnly. 'I'm so happy to have made it to the end. I've learnt so much here. That's why I'm delighted to say, I am a Faithful.'

Ruby steps forwards and pauses. 'I am so proud to have made it this far, even though I rejoined the game late. It's been a pleasure to get to know each and every one of you. I'm so proud of us, and I am a Faithful.'

Everyone cheers and hugs. You did it!

YOU HAVE WON.

BONUS GAME

BOP

Players: at least three, ideally seven or more

One person is nominated the Bopper and everyone else stands in a <u>circle</u>, facing inwards.

The Bopper looks around the other players, turning around, slowly choosing which to 'bop'.

After some time, the Bopper points at the player of their choosing and shouts 'Bop'.

The 'bopped' player must immediately duck down.

At that point, each of the two players on *either side* of the 'bopped' player race to point at the other and shout 'Bop'.

The Bopper in the middle declares who was first to shout 'Bop'; the other player leaves the game. The Bopper is able to declare a draw, in which case play carries on.

If anyone shouts 'Bop' when it is not their turn, they leave the game.

When two players remain, the Bopper asks them to stand back to back.

Slowly, the Bopper instructs them to take a pace, then pauses . . .

At an unexpected moment, the Bopper shouts 'Bop' and the first player to turn around, point and shout 'Bop' is the winner.

After the game is finished, you sit for a while chatting with Ruby before you head upstairs. You ask each other: what on earth made us think we'd want to come to the Castle?

'I guess I like puzzles,' is Ruby's summary. 'When I do a crossword or even one of those big sudokus, it might take me a week. More. There's no point rushing these things. As I see it, anyway.'

- Turn to **89**.

Almost immediately after leaving the library, you bump into River, who asks if she can join you. You've noticed that she's a reliable morale booster. That doesn't mean she's Faithful, you remind yourself, but she is definitely decent company.

'Not to talk about who might be a Traitor, just to talk about something else for a change,' she offers, 'though I'm prepared to say that I'm pretty sure you're a Faithful!'

It's always a nice feeling whenever anyone says anything like that.

As you cross the lawn, Nina and Deb are deep in conversation, trying, it seems, to make each other laugh. It's a nice thing to see, and they look like they've known each other for ages.

You've passed them when Deb bursts into giggles and you're pretty sure you hear her say, 'Oh, stop it, Gran!'

River looks at you and a part of you wonders if her look says: 'Did you hear that too?' But for some reason neither of you speaks. You worry for a moment that this makes you look suspicious. But you've learnt never to play a hand too soon in this Castle.

However, it's only a part of you. You must have imagined it. Mustn't you?

- Turn to **103**.

Right. Here goes nothing.

'I made the decision when I came in here that I would be entirely myself. One hundred per cent honest. That's who I am. And you've all asked me questions and I've told you what I honestly think. I haven't been guiding anything. I've just been honest. To me that's the mark of a Faithful. But can everyone around the table say the same?' You look at David, almost enjoying the melodrama of it. 'Dave, is there anything you'd like to share with the group?'

He looks down at the table, shamefaced. Then it all comes spilling out. How he's lied. How there is no pub and how sorry he is.

Deb and Rakayah look heartbroken. Deb says, 'The one thing I can't stand in life is a liar.' You don't need to do any more. The conversation leads inexorably to the inevitable question – if he was lying about that, what else might he be lying about? When it's time to write a name, almost everyone, you included, writes down David's name.

He stands in front of everyone.

'Well, David,' says the Host. 'You have been chosen to leave. But are you Faithful or a Traitor?'

'I just want to say again to everyone how sorry I am that I lied. But I'm a Faithful.'

There is an audible gasp and Deb shouts out, 'Nooooooo!'

- Turn to **241**.

'I was utterly shocked when I heard this story from Gregg earlier,' you say. Your voice is calm and confident. 'And I think we're probably all feeling pretty similar. The first thing is that Nina, who we all loved and trusted, has been lying to us the entire time. On top of what happened with Deb, it's just too much. If that isn't the marker of a Traitor, I don't know what is. And if you knew you were lying, why would you draw attention to it by going on about plants so much!' A few people, clearly hurt by Nina's lie, nod along and mutter agreement.

'But the second thing is that there's clearly something a bit fishy about how Gregg has told us. Whether it was genuinely a mistake or . . . something else, I'm not sure. But I think he's certainly held back this story for dramatic effect, and at best that's clumsy and at worst cruel.'

Gregg reads the room and decides his best course of action is to play the fool. He apologises and explains it was just him being stupid and overthinking things. Nina tries to make her case but her anger makes it feel like she's lashing out, and she forgets to even defend her original lie. Tim and River sadly and regretfully say they feel disappointed in Gregg but they feel more let down by Nina. Anna agrees and things are set.

As the names are revealed, it's looking pretty even between you, Gregg and Nina. But as River and Tim both hold up Nina's name one after the other, it's her by one vote.

As your Host brings her forwards to tell the room if she's Faithful or a Traitor, there is still a tremor of emotion in her voice.

'Well, since we're being honest . . . I'm a Traitor.'

The room erupts with excited chatter. Gregg looks sad but relieved to be staying. Tim just looks shocked.

YOU HAVE BANISHED A TRAITOR.

- Turn to **58**.

220

That's not the right answer. If you think we can say for sure that a truth-teller is not pointing at a liar, you have not been thinking methodically enough. Return to **228**.

221

'You're absolutely right, River. I have been keeping a secret,' you say. 'But it's not that I'm a Traitor. Actually, the night before last, the Traitors attempted to seduce me into becoming a Traitor. And I turned them down.' The room is stunned into silence as people consider the implications of this.

Gabriel is looking especially thoughtful. 'That would explain Teddy!' he says excitedly. 'How he seemed to change at that specific moment.'

'Very interesting, but how do we know that's true?' says River, clearly hoping that you'll carry the can tonight. 'There's no proof. Any of us could say that.'

'River,' you say. 'I can say with complete confidence, I am not creative enough to come up with a lie like that.' You're not sure if it's a compliment that this argument lands so well. But it seems to have taken the spotlight off you and back onto River and Tim.

Ruby chips in, 'Look, when it comes down to it, it's absolutely clear to me who is a Traitor and it's Tim. I tried to show you yesterday but you went with Anna and we banished another Faithful.'

Tim is smiling genially but it looks a bit forced this time. He tries to say that, to his mind, murdering Precious would have been the perfect move for Ruby to make to point the finger away from herself. River is nodding tentatively and Gabriel looks thoughtful too.

You can see that because of Nina, the idea that Tim is a similarly unexpected Traitor still makes a lot of sense to everyone. And where his niceness once seemed like his superpower, suddenly, without it, there are a few examples of people remembering him acting in a way that doesn't quite add up. Gregg chips in with a couple of key examples and now Tim's smile almost entirely falls away under the pressure. Ruby is like a star barrister and keeps him under relentless scrutiny. And like a bad witness, he crumbles. He is hostile and patronising and seems to be flailing around trying to blame everyone. First Gregg, then Ruby, then even River. But nothing lands. It actually really starts to make sense to you.

As the names are revealed, Tim votes for Ruby, but the rest of you vote for Tim.

Your Host steps forwards.

'Let's see if you've got it right. Tim, are you Faithful or a Traitor?' By this time he's regained his composure somewhat.

'Well, everyone, it's truly been a pleasure getting to know every single one of you . . .' You watch as he looks all of you in the eye, though he barely even glances at River and then lingers on Gregg for longer than anyone else; you think you see something that looks like disappointment.

'But I have to tell you . . . I'm a Traitor.'

Ruby screams and the whole room lets out its breath.

YOU HAVE BANISHED A TRAITOR.

You are ushered into a room you have never been in before and handed a glass of champagne. Everyone is speculating that this is the end. Have you won, have you lost? Slowly you are led out to the front of the Castle where you can see firelight flickering.

- Turn to **51**.

222

Rakayah rattles on through more thoughts but, as you recall, part of her unpredictability entails seamless changes of subject. Without pausing to draw breath, she returns to the fact that Laure also mentioned Gregg and you but – and this of course comes as a great relief to you – insists that there is no reason to act on Laure's instinct. 'No offence, Teddy, but your face reading led us down some blind alleys. I respect you but you know I'm right.'

Instead, she insists, we should think about what we can see. She pauses and looks across at Elif. If this was deliberate, it is beautifully done, because suddenly the new topic is Elif and her book. So now it's Elif's turn to put up a defence and, truth be told, she is not the most persuasive of people.

In a moment that can only have been scripted by the gods who are on Rakayah's side, Elif tries to make a joke at her own expense, but her smile dies before it reaches her eyes.

And that is the moment you know her goose is cooked.

And when the names start to be written on the slates, you appear a couple of times, as does Gregg. But it's Elif whose name receives the most votes. Almost everyone locks onto the combination of book and funny smile. Yet again you are struck by how all it takes is for someone to sow the seed confidently enough and the whole room follows their lead.

For all you are relieved that you won't be leaving, your heart sinks when she – very gracefully – says that as a Faithful, it pains her to say goodbye.

Still, as you later wait for sleep to come, you wonder: what would have happened if you hadn't let Rakayah carry on talking.

YOU HAVE BANISHED A FAITHFUL.

- Turn to **59**.

223

There is a party atmosphere as everyone revels in the triumph of finally banishing a Traitor. All anyone can talk about is how strange it was that Rakayah managed to avoid suspicion until you said what you'd said. You smile and accept the acclaim. But inside you are worried. Is it beyond the Traitors to react immediately with revenge and murder you immediately?

As the gong sounds and you slip upstairs to your room, you wonder what will happen. The night is full of creaking floorboards. You close your eyes, wondering if this will be your time, but revelling in the feeling of taking down a Traitor.

- Turn to **245**.

You are invited out to the front steps of the Castle where your Host is waiting for you.

'So, you have banished a Traitor. You must all be feeling pretty happy with yourselves. But I have another surprise for you. Call it a reward. There will be no Conclave and therefore no murder tonight.' You all cheer spontaneously. 'But in exchange, after tomorrow's Mission, you will decide when the game ends. When you are absolutely confident there are no remaining Traitors, simply tell me and we will end the game. Either when there are three finalists left or you unanimously decide, the game will end. But remember, if there is even a single Traitor amongst you, the Traitors will win.'

Back inside, Ruby leads the celebrations, as she tops up people's drinks. But you are shaken. Tonight was too close for comfort.

At one point there's a silence, and you tell them that you didn't want to use it in the Round Table because it would have looked like you were saying it to manipulate people, but they need to know that the night before last the Traitors tried to seduce you and you said no.

The room is shocked, then Gabriel points out that makes total sense with what happened with Teddy. He asks if anyone else has been offered the same deal and everyone shakes their heads. You are relieved that people seem to agree that you sharing this information now is a sign that it's true, as there's no real angle for you to make up a lie in this context. It even seems to perk people up a bit, as they rage against the devious tricks of the Castle.

Still, there is a palpable sense of relief when the gong sounds and it's time to head up to your room.

You fall asleep turning over the various permutations of Traitors in your head, and are, you think, relieved to wake to a pale sun. You have made it to the final day.

- Turn to **113**.

225

After the Mission, you spend some time with Rakayah and Teddy.

Teddy is again expounding his theories on what he would do if he were a Traitor, and you're distracted trying to get straight in your head whether this is how a crypto guy is likely to think and talk, or a strategy to keep ramming home the idea that he's not a Traitor.

Risky, you think to yourself. But then risk-taking is one of Teddy's pet topics.

'I'm not saying this is definitely true – necessarily – but if you're a Traitor, you're gonna be wary of someone who comes up with theories, thoughts, scenarios. You're more likely to keep in the game, I dunno, someone like . . . River. She's more of a watcher, you know? Solid strategy. I like her.'

Rakayah – still more subdued than usual – isn't sure. 'I dunno. It must have been tough. Murdering anyone, I mean, but people liked Laure.' She pauses and looks at you. 'In general.'

You're unsure of your best next move so you play it cool.

'What do you mean?' you ask.

'Well,' replies Rakayah, 'just that I heard you and her had beef.'

Oh dear. A rumour has clearly started. And inflated. This close to

Round Table, you need to make sure this isn't what half the room are thinking about as they go in.

What do you do?

- Call out Gregg in his absence. Turn to **305**.

- Stand your ground and debunk the rumour. Turn to **142**.

226

You return to your room and get ready for bed. You are tired but satisfied with your day. You met a lot of people and gave a good account of yourself. You feel like you got the balance right and you are clearly a useful ally without having painted a target on your back.

As you fall asleep that evening, you hear a faint hissing. A cat? Too low and measured for a cat. From the corner of your eye, you see purple smoke coming through your keyhole. As you fall asleep, you curse your loud confidence in the bar, which must have established you as a threat.

YOU HAVE BEEN MURDERED.

To play this day again, please return to **1**. Better luck next time!

On your way around the Castle, you bump into Amrit and Isla, who are heading towards you.

'How are the steps gang?' calls out Amrit happily.

'Oh, you know,' you say. 'Obsessed with how you can tell a Traitor from how they smile.'

'Oh really,' says Isla. 'How's that?'

'Apparently, their smile will stop at the eyes,' you say. 'Like this.' Then you do your best Terminator face.

'We were actually just saying that we need to be thinking more about what people are doing and less about what they're saying,' says Amrit. 'We reckon a Traitor will be watching everyone loads. Also, we reckon that the Traitors will have to start bumping off good eggs soon, just to even the odds a bit if they're ever up against someone at Round Table.'

'And Amrit reckons that means that I'm going to murder him!' says Isla delightedly, both of them laughing. It feels good to see two people with such an obviously real relationship in the middle of so much guessing and second-guessing. You smile as you watch them walk off, like two best friends in a school playground.

All too soon though it's time to head inside, where your Host is waiting for you.

'It's Mission time again.' You have to admit, you've actually grown quite fond of these moments when everyone has the same aims. For once, you can just let your guard down and only worry about whether or not you're going to muck up the Mission.

- Turn to **96**.

MISSION

WHO'S LOOKING AT WHO?

Your Host welcomes you to the library. You are told that Gabriel, River and you are to stand in the middle of the room.

The others naturally form a kind of loose circle around you. Great, you think to yourself wryly. Scrutiny always gives you an advantage in this world.

'River is a liar . . .' announces your Host.

You're not the only one to gasp.

'But, but . . .' splutters Tim.

'I knew it!' snaps Gabriel.

'. . . for the purposes of this activity only.'

Gabriel looks ashamed for a moment, then grins and says, 'I knew that too!' Laughter.

'And Gabriel,' continues your Host, 'is a truth-teller.'

'I am in real life, and also for the purposes of this activity,' quips Gabriel.

Gabriel is instructed to point at you. You are instructed to point at River.

'The question,' concludes your Host, 'is whether a truth-teller is pointing at a liar.' Eyes dart around, most of them on you.

'A liar,' you add hastily, 'for the purposes of this activity.'

What do you think the answer is?

- *Yes, certainly, a truth-teller is pointing at a liar.* Turn to **299**.

- *No, actually, a truth-teller is not pointing at a liar.* Turn to **220**.

- *We can't tell whether a truth-teller is pointing at a liar.* Turn to **158**.

- If you are Faithful, turn to **19**.

- If you are a Traitor, turn to **76**.

229

'Up until a few nights ago, I wouldn't have ever thought it in a million years,' you say, 'then Nina happened. I'm not saying I'm totally agreeing with you. But I'm not ruling it out either.' You feel proud of your reasoning. River was right, the trick is just to pretend you don't know that you're a Traitor.

'Ooh, careful with those splinters in your bum from sitting on that fence!' says Ruby. You can't help but warm to her. She's forthright and charming. But she's dangerous. You can see why you couldn't murder her, but you wish she wasn't in the game.

'Let's both just keep an eye on both of them,' she says. And you nod.

'Right. We should go join up with the others,' Ruby says. 'Before they start to gossip!'

Just then, word comes around that it's time for the Mission.

• Turn to **252**.

230

After the Mission, you all go and sit outside, looking out over the gardens, remembering those that have left the Castle.

The names that rush through your mind make it feel like a pinball machine. Not so long ago, you were trying to work out what Irwin was thinking, to analyse Amrit, to suss out Deb. You haven't even had a moment to give Tim another thought since the dust settled.

And yet still it goes on. You think of Anna and her numbers, Jorge and his memory, David and his imaginary pub. You wonder what Nina is doing, and Teddy. You even slightly miss Laure (or maybe not).

- Turn to **73**.

231

You write River. Ruby writes River. River has written Ruby's name. Your betrayal has paid off. River can't help but look at you with a look of grudging admiration. Clearly she didn't think you had it in you. Gabriel has written your name.

'River, you have been banished. Please tell us if you are Faithful or a Traitor.'

She steps forwards. 'This has been one of the most incredible experiences of my life. I'm proud to have made it this far. And I'm proud of you all. Because I am a Traitor.'

There is a mood of celebration as River is led away, and Gabriel and Ruby can't help but smile. You don't know if you have to bother any more, but you make sure to look suitably shocked at the news.

'So,' says your Host. 'The final three. Please step forwards and reveal whether you are Faithful or a Traitor.'

Gabriel steps forwards, smiling. 'When I came in here, I knew I just wanted to be me, whatever else happened. I wanted to be true to myself. And that's why I'm so happy to say that I am a Faithful.'

Ruby steps forwards and pauses. 'I am so proud to have made it this far, even though I rejoined the game late. It's been a pleasure to get to know each and every one of you. I'm so proud of us, and I am a Faithful.' They both turn expectantly to you, beaming. But something in your face must give it away, because their smiles freeze.

You can't help but smile. 'I've learnt so much being here and I've enjoyed meeting you all so much. That's why I'm genuinely sorry to say, I'm a Traitor.'

YOU HAVE WON.

232

'I'll go first this time,' you say. 'And it was actually something you said earlier, Ruby, that made me think of this.' She has a look of apprehension on her face. 'You said that you had been watching at the moment of banishment in case something stood out. And I suddenly worked out what it was that's been bugging me. When Tim was banished, he gave Gregg a look, a really specific kind of look. It wasn't anger, it was disappointment. The kind you might give a child who had disappointed you, or, perhaps, the more I think about it – a teammate who had turned on you. All of his behaviour since makes sense as a mixture of shame and caution.'

You watch as Ruby has a look of dawning realisation on her face. River says that she would never have believed it, but it makes so much sense.

Gregg tries to defend himself, explains that he's basically a simple, straightforward guy and this has all been too much for him. He tries to say that you are clearly distracting from your own behaviour, but you can see that your theory is stacking up for everyone else.

When the names are written, Gregg votes for you, but everyone else votes for him.

'Well then,' says your Host. 'Let's see whether you got this one right or not. Gregg, are you Faithful or a Traitor?'

'I wasn't lying that I'm a simple guy.' He looks everyone in the eye, one by one. You try to see if he lingers over anyone but he seems to give everyone the same amount of time and focus.

'But I am also . . . a Faithful.'

You slump your head on the desk. You were so sure and you were wrong.

YOU HAVE BANISHED A FAITHFUL.

- Turn to **307**.

You stay sitting at the Round Table, solemn and downbeat. You worry you're laying it on too thick but the finish line is in sight now, surely. Ruby touches your arm. 'It made sense to me too,' she says.

Your Host steps forwards. 'So you banished a Faithful. Why? Did you make the wrong decision or are there just no more Traitors left? The game is now in your hands. You now face a choice. If you all unanimously decide to end the game you can now. But if you believe there is a Traitor in your midst, you must banish again. You will need to join me out front for your final task. And a reminder. If there is even one Traitor among you, they have won. So eat, drink and be . . . wary?'

You realise there is one final chance to speak to the group and you all head into the drawing room, chatting about what this means. There are drinks and some food waiting on a table but you feel too churned up to eat.

River steps forwards. 'Well, I suppose one of us needs to say something. Personally, I'm certain on one person – me. And I'm ninety-five per cent sure on Gabriel. You two, I am really not sure about if I'm honest.' With horror, you realise that she is making a move against you. The sense of betrayal feels acute. After you were loyal in the last round. But that's the game.

There is that brief flicker of annoyance on Ruby's face as River speaks, which you wonder if she's aware of. She's primed to hit back. Should you take the lead, or let her do the dirty work?

Should you?

- Take the lead. Turn to **41**.

- Let Ruby do it. Turn to **183**.

234

River listens intensely as you explain that you've heard pretty much everyone's name mentioned so far this morning, and that you'd be willing to bet yours is too when you're not in the room.

'I think we have to try and get the spotlight on Gregg or Ruby,' she says. 'But, to be honest, I'm worried that Tim is going to be in the spotlight whatever happens after last night.'

Just then, she excuses herself and says she needs to go and get changed before Round Table. You have ten blissful minutes as you sit with your eyes closed, listening to the tick of a clock, before Gabriel puts his head around the door and says, 'It's time.'

You get up and walk towards the Round Table, your heart beating so loudly in your chest that you think people must be able to hear it.

- Turn to **265**.

235

'It was me,' you say. 'I was so shocked by what I heard, I couldn't not tell people. I'm sorry, Nina and Deb, if that makes things uncomfortable for you. But as I've said the whole way through, my policy is to be one hundred per cent honest while I'm here. And that means making hard choices sometimes.'

That seems to nip things in the bud. From this point onwards the conversation stays on Deb and Nina. It's clear that they are both well liked, and there is genuine sympathy for Nina who keeps wiping at her eyes. But there is a real sense of betrayal in the room and Deb is bearing the brunt of it. She tries to mount a defence that she isn't a Traitor based on how stupid it would be to keep this a secret if she was. But it's almost as if the room doesn't really care. They just want revenge.

When it's time to pick names, it's pretty much unanimous for Deb. She accepts the news graciously, nodding her head once.

'And now,' the Host says, 'it's time to tell us, are you Faithful or a Traitor?'

'Well, I'm genuinely sorry that we lied to you. But I wasn't lying about one thing. I am a Faithful.'

Gregg bangs the table with his fist and swears. The rest of the room slumps back in silence, the only sound Nina quietly sobbing.

YOU HAVE BANISHED A FAITHFUL.

- Turn to **304**.

236

You make your way to the end of the pack, where you find your-self standing next to Jorge (Folkestone, 60). He mutters under his

breath, 'I'm slightly regretting this now, are you?' You are, but try
to be upbeat. 'You can only be honest, can't you?'

'Now please stop moving!' The Host peers over at you. 'We asked
you to make a decision. And told you that every decision has con-
sequences. Well, here you are. This is a game where pride always
comes before a fall.' She gestures to Precious (Skye, 28) and Ruby
(York, 29). 'So I'm afraid, both of you are going home.'

There is an audible gasp. Some people are smiling, clearly thinking
it's a joke. But then Precious and Ruby are getting hugs. You notice
with mild annoyance that Rakayah (Dudley, 19) is crying, then feel
heartless.

You all turn your back on them and head into the Castle.

- Turn to **266**.

237

'I'm, like, actually pissed off now,' says Rakayah. 'These Traitors
are making a mockery of us.' Deb wisely keeps her head down, sitting with Gregg who is trying to reassure her that everything will
be fine. People sit in small groups, nursing drinks, waiting for the
gong to sound time to head up to their rooms.

The tapping of a glass.

'A toast to Isla and Amrit,' says Tim, standing slowly. 'They leave
with a genuine friendship. And after all, isn't that the real prize in
life.'

Everyone raises their glasses and you see a couple of people wiping
their eyes.

You go up to your room and for a moment wonder if tonight will be the night. But whatever the reason, you feel sanguine. If it's your time, it's your time.

- Turn to **283**.

238

'I'll go first this time,' you say. 'And it was actually something you said earlier, Ruby, that made me think of this.' She has a look of apprehension on her face. 'You said that it was hard to know what normal behaviour was in this environment. And that got me thinking about what is normal behaviour. And you know what isn't normal – one hundred per cent niceness all the time. Gabriel, you are either the nicest person in existence, or someone who has decided to craft a persona with only one note. A perfect Traitor.'

Gabriel is clearly shocked, and even hurt by your accusation. But he doesn't crumble. Instead he says that he has been utterly transparent and honest throughout the entire process. He says he is genuinely disappointed that you have attacked him like this, after some of your conversations earlier, and concludes that the only reason for it must be that you are desperately trying to distract people from your own increasingly erratic behaviour. He says that this behaviour has made up his mind. You are a Traitor.

Ruby is also surprised by this sudden aggression on your part. River agrees that this feels like it bears little relationship to conversations you had earlier. Gregg can clearly see which way the wind is blowing and says something vague about seeing everyone's point of view.

When the names are written, you vote for Gabriel, just for consistency as much as anything else, but everyone else votes for you. To come so close but so far from winning burns. You can't help but feel you came to a point where you could have grasped victory, but clutched madly, in the crucial final seconds, at the wrong thing.

'I am . . . a Faithful,' you say.

YOU HAVE BEEN BANISHED.

To play this day again, please turn to **113**. Better luck next time!

239

'Right, you lot,' says your Host. 'Frankly, so far you have an appalling record of finding Traitors. Will that change tonight, or will you continue to punch yourselves in the face?'

River is acting as a sort of chair. 'It's the worst part of the day,' she had said earlier, 'so we need to make sure it's not even worse – no one likes to banish a Faithful.'

The theories so far have included:

The concept of 'alliances'. Amrit and Isla are the obvious example. Teddy, who takes the opportunity once again to remind everyone that you only make money at crypto if you know how people think, insists that they must either both be Traitors or both Faithfuls. Amrit says he certainly hopes so, which gets a laugh. Isla disagrees: she says Amrit is a mate and she hopes they'll be mates once this is all over – 'but you just don't know, do you?'

Watching how people behave, Laure says she doesn't believe in ESP, but that if it is real, she would definitely have it. Jorge gently interjects that he definitely doesn't believe in extra-sensory perception because of his medical training.

'Didn't know they covered that in dentistry,' says Nina to herself, and you can't help but snort quietly.

Laure says that she can tell who is tense this evening. She mentions Rakayah, Gregg and, to your dismay, you. You have been blind-sided. You have kept your head down the entire day.

Rakayah speaks on behalf of all three of you: 'Of course we're all tense. We've gotta banish someone, someone's gonna get murdered; if I'm tenser than anyone else it's because I don't have a plan. I'm just me.'

You're not sure what the others will make of this. Rakayah has, in part, dismissed Laure's claims of ESP, but she's only mentioned herself as not having a plan. On the other hand, whether or not she's a Traitor, you think people are looking at her like she might be.

Should you let Rakayah dig a deeper hole, or do you run the risk of guilt through association?

What do you do?

- Pipe up and defend yourself. Turn to **159**.

- Let her talk in the hope that she continues to draw attention to herself. Turn to **222**.

BONUS GAME

MIND READER

Players: four or more

One player is appointed the Mind Reader and leaves the room.

The other players decide on a Rule. This might be 'the player on my left' or 'the player who is next tallest compared to me if we were put in order of height'.

The Mind Reader returns and sits in the middle of a circle formed by the other players.

The Mind Reader chooses any player and asks them a question about themselves.

That player must *give the answer which would be given by the player determined by the Rule* (that is, by the player on their left, by the next tallest player, etc.).

Players may need to guess their answers, but should always give an answer.

If an answer is inaccurate, any player who knows that

it is inaccurate may shout 'Switcheroo', at which point everyone except the Mind Reader must change places.

The Mind Reader's job is to identify the Rule.

You notice that even Gregg started to come out of his shell a bit during the game and there were no confrontations. But all too soon, it is time to head to the Round Table.

- If you are Faithful, turn to **214**.

- If you are a Traitor, turn to **211**.

After a shocked group talk about David and his fictional pub, and the fact you've sent another Faithful home, several people come up to you and apologise for doubting you. Your speech really seems to have landed and you feel you were right to make yourself visible today.

As you settle into bed that night, you hear your window open and the sound of something sliding in and hissing. As you feel a sharp pain in your ankle, you realise that you have made yourself too visible to the wrong people.

YOU HAVE BEEN MURDERED.

To play this day again, please turn to **202**. Better luck next time!

'Well, here we are,' your Host says. 'By the end of the day, we will know if it is the Faithful or the Traitors who have won the game. But first you must choose one of you to be banished now. So go to it!'

You all look around the room, everyone waiting for someone else to go first but no one wanting to break the silence. You decide that you are going to go first, but what should you say? Ruby has been such an active presence since she came back to the Castle. But if she's a Traitor, she's effectively taken out two of her own. Surely there'd have been visible bad blood there? The one person you've never really suspected is Gabriel, but couldn't that equally be the marker of an expert Traitor. And thinking about something Ruby said earlier, was there some detail from the last two banishments that you couldn't put your finger on that was setting off an alarm with Gregg?

What do you do?

- Throw doubt about Ruby. Turn to **292**.

- Question whether anyone can be as nice as Gabriel seems to be. Turn to **238**.

- Point the spotlight at Gregg. Turn to **232**.

'Hey, wait for me,' you call. Gabriel turns, looking startled. Then smiles when he sees you. 'I was just going to collect my thoughts before the day kicks off, but I know you won't throw lots of theories at me, so you can join me.'

You both sit in companiable silence for a while.

'I have basically no idea who is a Traitor,' says Gabriel finally. 'Apart from that I know I'm not, and I'm pretty sure you're not. But the other three, I have no idea. When I'm with them, I think they're definitely not, and then I realise that's exactly what a good Traitor would make you think. Whatever happens, someone we've trusted has been lying to us. So who knows!'

It feels nice that at least one person has your back and you agree that you're sure Gabriel is Faithful too, with just the tiniest voice in the back of your head saying that's exactly what a Traitor would be doing – forming multiple alliances and flattering people into reciprocating. You chat for a bit about Gregg still seeming quiet since the revelation that Tim was a Traitor. You both think it's likely that he saw Tim as a mentor figure.

'Well, I'll leave you to it,' you say, and Gabriel salutes goodbye.

- Turn to **167**.

'I don't believe it, I just don't believe it,' says Elif.

You sit in shock between Tim and Teddy in the bar, as people mutter among themselves.

'I was so sure,' says Teddy.

'Don't be too harsh on yourself, lad,' says Tim, patting his hand. 'Anyone can make a mistake.'

As you sit, you realise how quickly people can turn at Round Table. The evening is a blur of names and faces, as you try to learn more about the people you're meeting. You talk to Anna about your maths teachers when you were growing up, and sit with Gregg and Deb as they discuss where they like to go out at home. At one point, Rakayah makes Jorge sing a song to Isla and Amrit, and everyone has to admit he's surprisingly good.

The gong signals that it's time for bed.

- Turn to **172**.

245

DAY 7

Anna is counting down as people arrive to breakfast. You watch her as you sip your coffee.

'You do know we're all doing that in our heads, Anna?' teases Gregg. 'You don't actually need to be an actuary to run the numbers at this point.'

The funny thing is: this is the wrong day to be counting. As Nina,

Jorge and Gregg file in, Anna counts 'Two, one, zero,' and just as everyone is working out that it must be Deb who's been murdered, in she files.

There is general bewilderment. Everyone left at Round Table is here this morning, too.

Your Host explains: 'Last night, the Traitors did not carry out a murder.'

The bewilderment rapidly turns to cheers.

Gregg has a theory. 'So I reckon that either normal rules don't apply when we banish a Traitor. Or, they tried to murder someone and they had a Shield. But then why would you pick someone who might have had one? I'm bad at maths, but surely there was someone they could have gone for who definitely didn't?'

You want to agree but are aware that talking about this logically will lead to the conclusion that the only ones who would know that are the remaining Traitors, however many are left.

'Well, the only people who know that are the Traitors,' says Nina quietly. 'And I know I'm not one of those.'

'What are they up to?' asks Tim. You expect Teddy to leap in as usual with his theory, but he is sitting there nodding along.

The mood is undeniably jolly – though you can't be the only one wondering what the Traitors are up to – and it's a slightly larger than expected group that files out.

What do you do?

- Head upstairs for a bit of quiet time. Turn to **74**.

- Head to the drawing room for a chat. Turn to **47**.

246

You fill your glass deliberately slowly and, as you hoped, someone strikes up a conversation. It's Gregg. 'Worst bit of the day, this,' he reckons, 'though I did say that about Round Table too.' He laughs at his own inconsistency. 'And I guess being murdered is no picnic.'

You watch who's coming in and who isn't. Most people seem anxious. Isla's looking past some groups – checking to see if Amrit's here, you tell Gregg. Nina and Teddy are the last to arrive (they come at the same time), and now there can be no doubt who won't be playing today.

- Turn to **155**.

247

'I was actually just trying to work out if it was going to be harder or easier for you two, and I really couldn't make my mind up,' you say.

'I know, right!' says Precious. 'We were talking about that this morning. There are pros and cons. But who knows.'

The conversation moves on. The hive mind, if there is such a thing, alights on a topic that can't really be contentious: who has left the Castle (and won't be making a shock re-entry). It's funny to realise you haven't thought about, say, Steve-O or Elif for some time. You don't feel bad, though; you quite simply don't have the brain space.

- Turn to **192**.

You're not sure if you've run out of the energy to lie, or whether it just feels like the right moment for the truth, but you take a deep breath.

'Well, Gregg, I'm pretty sure there are some people who think this is how a Traitor might act if they'd taken out one of their own. But I would say there's an equally strong school of thought that you're just upset like all of us that Nina was a Traitor.' He looks at you and even that small moment of kindness seems to have rejuvenated him.

'Thank you for your honesty,' he says.

Up ahead, Gabriel calls back, 'Everyone's going to play a game in the library!' You both quicken your pace to catch up with the others.

- Turn to **240**.

You chip in defending Tim, admitting that while you have heard his name a few times today, you've heard Anna's just as often. You can see from the way that Gabriel, Gregg and River are nodding along that you made the right call. Tim has made it a straight popularity contest and he's almost certainly going to win. At this stage, you can vote with the Traitors and it won't look strange. The perfect result for you. Ruby harrumphs and Precious sits there with her arms crossed but then it's time for the vote.

As the names are revealed, Anna, Ruby and Precious both vote for Tim, restating their original reasoning but the rest of you vote for Anna. River goes first and says, 'I just didn't hear that passion when you were defending yourself that I'd expect if you were a Faithful.' Everyone else gives some version of that too.

Your Host steps forwards. 'Let's see if you've got it right. Anna, please tell the room, are you Faithful or a Traitor?'

She stands in front of you with a calm smile on her face.

'The numbers never lie. I am a Faithful.'

There is a collective groan. 'I told you,' says Ruby in disgust.

YOU HAVE BANISHED A FAITHFUL.

- Turn to **78**.

250

Gabriel, Anna and Nina are still sitting outside at one of the tables.

'Pull up a pew,' says Nina. 'We're trying to work out if even this place would be twisted enough to send one or both of Precious and Ruby in as a Traitor.' You admit that you've been thinking that too and come to the conclusion that you can't rule anything out.

'The real problem is,' says Anna, 'we have nothing to benchmark their behaviours against.'

'Well,' says Gabriel, 'I feel pretty confident that Ruby isn't a Traitor. That question she asked last night pretty much directly led to Teddy's demise. So unless Traitors have started knocking each other off, that feels like a strong clue to me. Precious, I feel like I haven't met her enough to make my mind up. I am not incurious about Gregg, if I'm honest.' Everyone nods along at that.

The conversation moves on to nostalgia around childhood summers gone by, which were always sunny and seemed to last forever. You're getting too hot, so you say goodbye and head inside.

- Turn to **216**.

251

You and Nina find Gabriel and Tim sitting on a bench overlooking the grounds, which somehow look more magisterial than ever. As usual, Nina is testing herself by listing the Latin names of every plant she can see. You suddenly feel a long way from everything you're used to. But there's a game to play.

Gabriel is musing on possible reasons for the Traitors murdering Laure. 'Were you there when she said she was on the verge of a breakthrough? I mean, I'm not saying she would necessarily have been right—'

'God rest her soul,' interjects Tim with a twinkle in his eye.

Gabriel smiles, '—but it would have been interesting to think about who she was developing theories about.'

'I never heard her talk about anyone in particular,' offers Nina.

'Oh, I did,' chips in Tim. 'Last time I spoke to her, she was interested in Jorge. About how he seems to know everything, or rather remember it. Her theory was that in his job, he needs to remember lots of little things about patients to make it feel personal.'

You realise that you haven't really been paying much attention to Jorge, as he always seems to be across the room, beaming with those perfect choppers of his.

Conversation turns to last night. Like you, Gabriel had wondered why Deb seemed to be taking so much personal responsibility for the banishment of Isla. 'We voted, after all. Deb didn't force anyone's hand.'

And he adds another observation. Rakayah, who often has a big reaction to every banishment and murder, didn't seem to have any response at all at breakfast.

Now he mentions it, you think he's right.

'That's interesting,' says Tim. 'Ooh, look, up there. Is that a buzzard?' You look up where a shadow is circling lazily high above. You think of making a joke but you don't.

- Turn to **132**.

MISSION

THE DUCHESS'S MESSENGERS

You need: pencil and paper (or play without – see below)

Players: ideally at least four

One player should be appointed the Duchess.

The player to her left is the First Messenger. They think up a one-sentence message for the Duchess. It could be silly, alarming, startling, surreal . . .

That player whispers the Message to the Second Messenger – the player on their left – making sure that nobody else can hear.

The Second Messenger then draws the best visual representation of the message that they're capable of. Words are frowned upon in this illustration.

This is now passed on to the player to the left of the Second Messenger (the Third Messenger). They must study the illustration and come up with a single sentence that they believe conveys what they think they're looking at.

This chain continues – whispering and illustrating – until we return to the Duchess.

First, the Duchess either repeats the message (if the player before her delivered a message in the form of a sentence) or makes a new single sentence based on the illustration that was provided by the previous player.

The Duchess additionally tries to guess what the original message might have been.

Points are assigned as you wish on the basis of creativity, imagination and ingenuity.

> **Variant:** *Pencil and paper is not used and subsequent Messengers deliberately change one piece of information when passing on the message.*

> **Advanced variant:** *Players combine the pencil-and-paper version with the deliberate changing of information.*

After the Mission, you are told by your Host that there will be no trip to the Armoury today, which is met with nervous eye contact and muttering.

- If you are Faithful, turn to **2**.

- If you are a Traitor, turn to **151**.

'I'm really only saying this to check in with everyone else, but I feel like I've noticed a bit of a change in Tim over the last couple of days.'

As soon as you've said it, you realise your error. Tim is utterly charming, as he explains that he was just so upset by the last couple of banishments that he's gone into his shell a bit. Everyone offers their sympathy.

Then Teddy looks at you sharply. 'I don't know about anyone else but it's not so much a change, more that you're always in the frame but somehow never get banished. And pretty much every time, we banish the wrong people. Maybe we need to stop making that mistake.'

You are shocked by the sharpness of his tone, and though you try to point out that you were actually the one who basically got rid of Rakayah, it sounds thin even to your ears. Gradually the room warms to Teddy's version of events and it's like dominoes falling as it is time for people to vote. You notice with a grim smile that even Precious and Ruby have been swayed by his argument.

It is no relief to see the shock in their eyes when you stand and tell them you're Faithful.

YOU HAVE BEEN BANISHED.

To play this day again, please turn to **295**. Better luck next time!

254

As you speak, people lean in to listen. After spending the day second-guessing yourself, this feels good, like the first time you've actually been yourself. And people seem to be agreeing with you. Rakayah clearly sees you as someone to look up to and is nodding along in admiration. 'That's really smart. I hadn't thought of it like that.'

What do you do?

- Carry on, you're on a roll. Establishing yourself early like this is going to be key to building cachet within the group. Turn to **203**.

- Row back a bit. After all, no one likes a motormouth. Turn to **154**.

255

Ruby makes to leave but then reverses as if she's forgotten something. 'I wanted to ask you privately, as I feel like you'll give me a straightforward answer.'

'Thanks,' you say. 'I think.' Would she be this direct if she suspected you? Maybe she just wants to see how you respond under pressure.

'Do you think they've murdered Precious to get to me?' Phew.

'What do you mean?'

'I went after Tim and even though he was able to turn the room, he's still my number one suspect. The way I see it, Gregg is too dim to have it in him. Gabriel is either a genius sociopathic Traitor, or just actually is that nice. River couldn't give out more Faithful vibes if she was wearing a white cloak, which actually makes me think I need to watch her a bit more. I feel like you're definitely a Faithful. So that leaves Tim as my only definite. We have to pay close attention to everything Tim and River do.'

You decide that you can't push back against both of them, that would look odd. So which one should you go with; who would it be better to point the finger at? You think carefully about how to respond.

What do you do?

- Agree that Tim is in your thoughts too. Turn to **229**.

- Say that actually River feels like a better bet. Turn to **35**.

256

'I'm sorry but I have to step in here. I've been thinking about it all day. And River just doesn't make any sense to me. Whereas everything that's been said about Tim makes perfect sense.' He matches your gaze coolly and is it your imagination, or do you see even a hint of admiration in his eyes?

He tries to say that, to his mind, murdering Precious would have been the perfect move for Ruby to make to point the finger away from herself. River is nodding tentatively and Gabriel looks thoughtful too.

You can see that because of Nina, the idea that Tim is a similarly unexpected Traitor still makes a lot of sense to everyone. And where his niceness once seemed like his superpower, suddenly, without it, there are a few examples of people remembering him acting in a way that doesn't quite add up. Gregg chips in with a couple of key examples and now Tim's smile almost entirely falls away under the pressure. Ruby is like a star barrister and keeps him under relentless scrutiny. And like a bad witness, he crumbles. He is hostile and patronising and seems to be flailing around trying to blame everyone. First Gregg, then Ruby, then even River. But nothing lands.

As the names are revealed, Tim votes for Ruby, but the rest of you vote for Tim.

Your Host steps forwards.

'Let's see if you've got it right. Tim, are you Faithful or a Traitor?' By this time he's regained his composure somewhat.

'Well, everyone, it's truly been a pleasure getting to know every single one of you . . .' Is it you, or does he linger on you and River for longer than anyone else; will the others have noticed?

'But I have to tell you . . . I'm a Traitor.'

Ruby screams and the whole room lets out its breath.

YOU HAVE BANISHED A TRAITOR.

You are ushered into a room you have never been in before and handed a glass of champagne. Everyone is speculating that this is the end. Have you won, have you lost? Slowly you are led out to the front of the Castle where you can see firelight flickering.

- Turn to **63**.

257

As you sit around the table, glancing nervously at each other, you catch Nina's eye and give her a quick smile. To your left, Teddy (South London, 24) and Luke are having a conversation about which high-performance podcasts they listen to, which involves lots of men who have dogs' names.

Then your Host steps forwards.

'Now, it is time to choose the Traitors. Please put on the blindfold in front of you.'

You feel the material cool against your eyelids, the sound of twenty people trying not to breathe too loudly.

'If your destiny is to be a Traitor, I will tap you on the shoulder.'

You hear footsteps and creaking floorboards. The sound of someone pausing regularly. Then they are behind you.

You wait for the feel of a hand touching your shoulder, your heart beating fast. Worried that if it does, you'll make a noise and reveal yourself. But it never comes. You sit there in darkness for what feels like hours but must have been fifteen minutes, trying to sense any clue.

'Take your blindfolds off and look around. The Traitors are now among you.'

- Turn to **71**.

258

DAY 9

Last time no one was murdered it was a huge shock. But this time it's clear that many of you were half expecting it. There's still an excited buzz in the room, as people seem to have rediscovered their appetites and their funny bones. Then your Host enters.

'Well, as I'm sure you've worked out by now, your successful work banishing a Traitor last night means there was no murder. Instead, they had the opportunity to seduce a Faithful to join their cause.'

You can't help but think back to last night's theory that the Traitors were somehow able to recruit a Faithful when one of them was banished. It was certainly the kind of devious thinking you had come to associate with this Castle.

Who would you choose?

The numbers are small enough now that you can watch everyone all at once.

You look first at Ruby, who is sitting with Precious and River. Ruby immediately distinguished herself with the question that ultimately led to the finger being pointed at Teddy. It would be a smart move to have seduced her. No one has any real way of knowing what she is like, so how would we notice any change. The same is true of Precious, though she seems less self-contained somehow, not someone you'd trust to keep solid under the pressure of being a Traitor.

River is easy company in general, and as ever you have to remind yourself that just because you like her doesn't mean she isn't a Traitor. Though she has never behaved in a way that has made you doubt her. But would becoming a Traitor change that?

At another table are Gregg and Gabriel. Gabriel could be a good choice: universally liked, genuinely nice, and always seems to read the room correctly, though that could be used for evil as much as for good. But would he even do it? Would he crumble on contact with the necessary deceit? Gregg doesn't really seem like he has it in him to be malign. Everything is visible on the surface.

And then there's the final group: Tim, Anna and Nina. Nina might have escaped banishment last night, but you remind yourself not to think of her as automatically Faithful. Anna might literally be a calculating type, but of that lot you'd probably try to recruit the affable Tim. Yet he seems unchanged: just as affable this morning as ever.

A thought strikes you: they didn't approach you. But then, you're not at all sure that *you* would choose you. You've been sailing pretty close to the wind throughout and it's only been a few hail Mary moments that have saved you. What would be the point of recruiting someone constantly on the edge of banishment already? Unless the whole point was that they wanted someone to sacrifice instead of them? It's like chess, but with the added complication that the pieces are allowed to lie about what they are.

- Turn to **212**.

259

You return to your room and get ready for bed. You are tired but satisfied with your day. You met a lot of people and feel confident you've done nothing to paint a target on your back.

At one point, you hear footsteps in the hall and the creak of a floorboard and sit up in bed, your heart pounding, but then they move on.

You sleep fitfully and wake to a thin, pale sun streaming through the curtains. You made it through the first night.

- Turn to **110**.

260

Again, you make the trip up the stone spiral staircase in your cloak.

You enter the chamber high in the rafters of the Castle. You all sit down, pulling your hoods back.

'That was too bloody close by half,' says Tim. River nods her head.

'Well done,' you say. 'Amazing speech.'

'Well, thanks to you both for the heads-up that River passed on earlier. I'd have been absolutely clueless if not. I can't believe everyone came for me like that suddenly.'

'Ok, we have to discuss who we murder tonight,' says River. 'For me it's only between three people: Gabriel, Ruby and Precious. What do you think?'

They turn to you. Who should you vote for?

- Gabriel. Turn to **270**.

- Ruby. Turn to **174**.

- Precious. Turn to **64**.

261

You find your way to the middle of the pack, where you briefly exchange glances with the others who are in the middle. 'I feel as if we have no idea of how good we're going to be at this, so it wouldn't feel right to stand at either end,' and then regret it when you receive fierce looks from anyone either side of you.

'Now please stop moving!' The Host peers over at you. 'We asked you to make a decision. And told you that every decision has consequences. Well, here you are. This is a game where pride always comes before a fall.' She gestures to Precious (Skye, 28) and Ruby (York, 29). 'So I'm afraid, both of you are going home.'

There is an audible gasp. Some people are smiling, clearly thinking it's a joke. But then Precious and Ruby are getting hugs. You notice with mild annoyance that Rakayah (Dudley, 19) is crying, then feel utterly heartless.

You all turn your back on them and head into the Castle.

- Turn to **266**.

You write Gabriel. Ruby writes River. River has written Ruby. Gabriel has written Ruby's name. You did it! Your pact worked and you and River have both made it through.

'Ruby, you have been banished. Please tell us if you are Faithful or a Traitor.'

She steps forwards. 'I am so proud to have made it this far, even though I rejoined the game late. It's been a pleasure to get to know each and every one of you. But I'm afraid you made a mistake. I am a Faithful.' A groan. You don't know if you even still need to but you make an effort to appear shocked as Ruby is quietly led away.

'So,' says your Host. 'The final three. Please step forwards and reveal whether you are Faithful or a Traitor.'

Gabriel steps forwards, smiling. 'When I came in here, I knew I just wanted to be me, whatever else happened. I wanted to be true to myself. And that's why I'm so happy to say that I am a Faithful.'

River steps forwards and pauses. 'This game has been one of the most amazing experiences of my life. I've loved meeting everyone. Which is why I'm really sorry to say, I'm a Traitor.'

Gabriel looks so crushed that you don't have the heart to spin it out for dramatic effect. You step forwards solemnly. 'This has been one of the most incredible things I've ever done. But I'm sorry, Gabriel. I am a Traitor too.'

You and River exchange a look. Team Traitor did it!

263

'But surely,' you say, 'that would be an incredibly obvious thing to do, wouldn't it?'

Teddy agrees with you: 'That's a pretty good point. Nice thinking. Plus I might feel stupid for saying this later but, you know, Tim? Just doesn't track for me.'

River's of the same mind. 'Yeah, 'cause you gotta think not just "Who would a Traitor murder?" but also "What would a Traitor think the rest of us would make of it?"'

Rakayah waves a hand in your direction. 'By that logic,' she says, looking you in the eyes, 'you're the person who's thinking most like a Traitor. I mean, it has to be said.'

You hope someone will leap to your defence, but no one does. Perhaps you shouldn't have shared your theory? After a short moment that feels like a long one, Gabriel says, 'To be fair, I was thinking the same way. And last time I checked I'm definitely not a Traitor!'

Laughter. You're relieved. But you're not keen on the fact that no one said that your being a Traitor 'just doesn't track' for them. Still, you noticed an appreciative nod from a number of people as you were making your point. It feels good to not be so passive.

You make your excuses after a while and say you're heading off for some fresh air. Alexis says she'll join you.

- Turn to **171**.

BONUS GAME

CAPTURE THE CASTLE: GUARDS

You need: deck of cards, phone with timer

Players: Town Crier, plus at least two others

Take from the deck two 2s (the Renegades) and two 10s (the Guards). Then add court cards (king, queen, jack) until there are three more cards than there are players.

One player is the Town Crier and should now read the text below.

I am shuffling the cards, and dealing one to everyone, including myself.

I am now placing the remaining cards face down in a row on the table.

Everyone, look at your card. If you have a 2, you are a Renegade, come to capture the castle. If you have a 10, you are a Guard. Everyone else is a member of the Royal Family.

Place your card face down, close to the three already on the table in a way that makes it clear whose is whose.

When I say, 'Let us dance!', the Masked Ball will commence. Everyone – including me – will close their eyes for a count of eight. During that time, any Renegades must open their eyes and clock each other.

Ready . . . Let us dance! One, two, three, four, five, six, seven . . . eight.

Everyone must open their eyes. When I say 'Guards, on Alert!', we will all again close our eyes for a count of eight. During that time, any Guards must open their eyes. They will see whether they are accompanied by another Guard. Any unallocated Guard cards must be in the middle.

Ready . . . Guards, on Alert! One, two, three, four, five, six, seven . . . eight.

Everyone must open their eyes. The King has heard that there may be a Renegade at his Masked Ball. In five minutes' time, he will have someone placed in the stocks. You have five minutes to debate whom to place in the stocks. Any of you may claim to have been assigned any of the identities: Royal Family, Renegade or Guard.

The time starts . . . now.

Set the timer, and then when the time is up . . .

After a count of five, we shall all vote. The player or players with the most votes shall be placed in the stocks.

If one or more Renegades is placed in the stocks, the Royal Family shall be declared victorious. If there were no Renegades, the Royal Family shall be declared victorious.

In all other situations, the Renegades shall be declared victorious. If you decide that the King should exhibit clemency, you should now agree to each vote for the player on your left, and nobody shall be placed in the stocks.

I shall now make the count of five. One, two, three, four, five.

NB: this game can be combined with other Capture the Castle games in the list of games at the start of the book, so long as the total number of cards is always topped up to three more than the number of players using members of the Royal Family.

After the game, you feel suddenly tired from keeping your secret, and decide to find somewhere quiet to gather your thoughts before Round Table.

- If you are Faithful, turn to **149**.

- If you are a Traitor, turn to **186**.

'And then there were six,' says your Host. 'You have made it this far. But whose race is run. Tonight you must banish another. Let the games begin.'

There is a pause. And then Ruby lays out both of her theories about River and Tim. She's pretty even handed but River is clearly taken aback and isn't expecting it. She agrees that last night you all came close to banishing Tim, but is quite gentle. She clearly feels she needs to deflect even more and, as she looks around the room with the look of a drowning person searching for something that floats, her eyes alight upon you. She wants some support.

What should you do?

- Help her out. After all, Tim is too far gone to come back from the suspicion. And it wouldn't be the worst thing in the world for her to owe you. Turn to **256**.

- You'd rather a wounded Tim left in the game. Get rid of River while you have the chance. Turn to **285**.

266

As you bound up the wide stairs and into the Castle, it's cool and smells of furniture polish. Your eyes slowly get used to the dimness and you see statues and corridors stretching off in various directions.

You are told you can explore the house and immediately people begin to form pairs and small groups. It feels a little bit like the first day of school all over again. Whatever happens, you're going to need allies, so you need to make a choice.

In one direction, a few people are heading towards an airy drawing room. It might be worth getting to know them, you think; some of them look like they know what makes people tick. On the other hand, it's a beautiful sunny day, you could head back outside and introduce yourself to the little gang that's collected on the steps, some of them leaning against pillars.

What do you do?

- Head to the drawing room. Turn to **112**.

- Head outside to the steps. Turn to **124**.

267

DAY 12

You find yourself oddly hungry at breakfast, arriving third with Gabriel and River already chatting away. It feels strange for there to be no tension over who arrives this morning. You had become so used to the combination of breakfast and drama. You sit down, aware again of how you have to concentrate on buttering your toast as someone who is Faithful would.

River says, 'I wonder why they did this. God, you could drive your-self mad, couldn't you? Is there some sort of sneaky ulterior motive at work? I'm just glad we're all here this morning!' She is so good at taking the lead without anyone noticing.

Your Host enters and addresses you.

'Good morning. I trust you slept well. A reminder that today is the final day. After the final Round Table, if you are confident there are no remaining Traitors, simply tell me and we will end the game. Remember, the game ends when there are three finalists left, but you have the option to end it before that if you all unanimously decide to. But if there is even a single Traitor amongst you, the Traitors will win. Until then, do try and relax.'

Breakfast breaks up and Gabriel heads down the corridor and River and Ruby head towards the main door.

What do you do?

- Head after Gabriel. Turn to **197**.

- Head outside with River and Ruby. Turn to **17**.

268

Alexis keeps trying to meet your eye. But you look down at the table.

Her face hardens. 'No, I'm sorry, but I'm not having this. I am a Faithful and I know I'm telling the truth. I know for a fact there are some people who can't say that. Dave, is there anything you'd like to share with the group?'

He looks down at the table, shamefaced. Then it all comes spilling out. How he's lied. How there is no pub and how sorry he is.

Deb and Rakayah look heartbroken. Deb says, 'The one thing I can't stand in life is a liar.' With a growing feeling of relief, you see how it becomes all anyone wants to talk about. You nod along and offer the odd word of agreement, but you sink happily into the background. The conversation leads inexorably to the inevitable question – if he was lying about that, what else might he be lying about? When it's time to write a name, almost everyone, you included, writes down David's name.

He stands in front of everyone.

'Well, David,' says the Host. 'You have been chosen to leave. But are you Faithful or a Traitor?'

'I just want to say again to everyone how sorry I am that I lied. But I'm a Faithful.'

There is an audible gasp and Deb shouts out, 'Nooooooo!'

YOU HAVE BANISHED A FAITHFUL.

- Turn to **308**.

'She said what?!' splutters Jorge.

'I'm pretty sure she said, "Stop it, Gran", like she was laughing too much.'

'Pretty sure or really sure?' says Tim. 'Because it's kind of a big deal.'

You feel you ought to commit; if you say you're not sure, you'll look like a rumour-monger.

'No,' you reply, 'I heard it, I just couldn't quite believe it.'

'Liars who lie about one thing in their life are more likely to lie about other things,' says Anna. 'There's masses of data to back that up. The old adage that your credit card company knows you're going to have an affair before you do is true. Human beings are creatures of habit.'

'I suggest we keep this to ourselves for now,' says Jorge. 'Let's watch them carefully and keep our powder dry.'

'Still, it is suspicious, isn't it?' says Tim.

Well, you did it. Now to stand back and watch the fireworks. You head back out to the corridor with a feeling of mild dread in the pit of your stomach.

The rest of the day passes without incident until it's time for Round Table.

- Turn to **191**.

'I think Gabriel would really put the cat amongst the pigeons,' you say. 'He's so quiet and has no beef with any of us. It'd send them into the day suddenly confused about everything. Plus he's so gentle and well liked they'll be really emotionally impacted.' River doesn't look convinced. 'At this stage, I'm thinking about who the threats are and Gabriel is probably at the bottom of my list. I know he trusts me and Tim. I'd much rather we went for Ruby or Precious. They're becoming a real threat.'

'Well, we can't go for Ruby,' says Tim. 'Not after she came for me so hard earlier. It'll look like straight revenge. But I do love the idea of breaking up Precious and Ruby. They're becoming a right little unit. Is it too obvious that we're doing that to get to Ruby though?'

You have an idea. 'Could we try and spin that it was exactly what a ruthless Traitor would do?' Both of them nod along. You all decide to murder Precious.

- Turn to **18**.

You let them argue among themselves, tit for tat. And it seems as if the fact you knew the secret hasn't really registered.

What really seems to have shocked people is that Nina has been lying the entire time. On top of what happened with Deb, it's just too much for people to take.

She tries to say that Gregg's behaviour is the really suspicious thing. But Gregg reads the room and decides his best course of action is to play the fool. He apologises and explains it was just him being stupid and overthinking things. Nina again tries to make her case but her anger makes it feel like she's lashing out, and she forgets to even defend her original lie. Tim and River sadly and regretfully say that while they may feel disappointed in Gregg, they actually feel let down by Nina. When Anna agrees, things are set.

As the names are revealed, it's looking pretty even between you, Gregg and Nina. But as River and Tim both hold up Nina's name one after the other, it's her by one vote.

As your Host brings her forwards to tell the room if she's Faithful or a Traitor, there is still a tremor of emotion in her voice.

'Well, since we're being honest . . . I'm a Traitor.'

The room erupts with excited chatter. Gregg looks sad but relieved to be staying. Tim just looks shocked.

YOU HAVE BANISHED A TRAITOR.

- Turn to **58**.

272

'He was just telling me he had a bit of a headache,' you offer.

Gabriel grins. 'You know the mad thing about being here? You can't just hear that someone has a headache, you have to ask yourself whether it's caused by the stress of having been a Traitor since the first night. I was all ready to share my theory that him and Precious have been suspiciously close since yesterday, but what do I know!'

You're certainly prone to this way of thinking too, though it sounds like not to the same degree as Gabriel. You tell him so.

He nods. 'I think it's also just how my mind works,' he agrees.

- Turn to **134**.

DAY 10

You're the first one in for breakfast this morning, though your ability to work out the significance of that is pretty minimal after a night spent tossing and turning. Should you immediately tell everyone what happened last night? You decide that the best course of action is never to give away a piece of information for free. Especially now it's not just about survival. Because if even one Traitor is still lingering when the dust settles, you and the other Faithfuls will go home with nothing in your pockets. Meanwhile, you can barely work out if you want toast or half a grapefruit.

The first knock at the door is Gregg. He looks as if he hasn't slept all night. Even though Nina had been a Traitor, she was a beloved part of the group and it's clearly hit him hard.

'Hooray,' he says, smiling ruefully. 'It's me.'

You smile genuinely. 'I'm not sure I have a hooray in me this morning, I'm afraid.'

There's another knock and Gabriel puts his head around the door, then Anna, then River, then Ruby, all with the same subdued sense of celebration, as people shuffle about fixing themselves coffee. You realise how glad you are that Ruby's still here. In such an intense environment, there's a value in someone calm – someone who doesn't tend to add to the drama.

Then the room realises that it's only Tim and Precious who aren't there. You suddenly wonder what you saying no to the Traitors last night will mean. Surely no murder?

There's a gentle knock on the door . . . and Tim comes around the corner, smiling. He scans the room and quickly works out who is missing. 'Oh, no . . .' But then there is a knock at the door and Precious enters, smiling. The room erupts into cheers.

'Well, last time this happened they recruited another Traitor,' says Gabriel. 'I'm happy to see you, Precious. But I can't help but feel a bit worried what this means too.'

'It does rather feel like that, doesn't it?' agrees Tim, sipping a cup of tea.

After breakfast, Gregg tells everyone he's going for a walk and sets off on his own. The others pair off: River, Precious and Ruby to sit on the steps and Gabriel, Tim and Anna to the library.

What do you do?

- Catch up with River, Precious and Ruby. Turn to **284**.

- Go with Gabriel, Tim and Anna. Turn to **7**.

274

River listens intensely as you explain that no one seems sure about anyone tonight, despite various theories.

'Well, exactly,' she says. 'All I know is that I'm a Faithful. I did have my eye on Ruby for a bit but Precious being murdered put paid to that . . . unless that was the whole point.' You nod and you both chat about Gregg and Gabriel.

She excuses herself and says she needs to go and get changed before Round Table. You have ten blissful minutes as you sit with your eyes closed, listening to the tick of a clock, before Gabriel puts his head around the door and says, 'It's time.'

You get up and walk towards the Round Table.

- Turn to **45**.

275

Correct! If you're in a group of two, it's obvious. If the other person's sniggering, you have a saucy chin. If they're not, you don't. And it applies in a group of three as well. And that's the interesting bit.

If neither Nina nor Gabriel had sniggered, you'd know your chin was clean. If only Nina had sniggered, you'd know your chin must be clean (otherwise Gabriel would have been sniggering too, and vice versa).

And if they're both sniggering? Well, remember that each of them said they didn't know whether their chin was saucy. But *if your chin was clean*, here's what would have happened:

Nina would have said to herself: '*If* my chin was clean, Gabriel would have been looking at *two clean chins*, and he wouldn't have sniggered. But no. He *did* snigger – so yes, *I do know*: I know that my chin must be saucy.'

And since Nina *didn't* say that, we know your chin wasn't clean. It was saucy. Well done.

- Turn to **21**.

MISSION

SMALL IS BEAUTIFUL

You need: deck of cards; some toothpicks or similar to use as tokens

Players: at least two (ideally more)

Everyone begins by offering a single toothpick.

Next, each player is dealt a card face down. Without looking at it, they hold it, facing outwards, against their forehead. So this is different to almost all other card games: you see all the other cards, but not your own.

The player on the dealer's left puts on the table one or more toothpicks as a claim that they have the lowest card (aces are low). Play continues in the same direction, and subsequent players may . . .

- **quit**: *if they think they don't have the lowest card, they may drop out, forfeiting any chance of winning the toothpicks (and may look at their card)*

- **match** *the number of toothpicks: they can stay in the running by adding the same number as the previous bidder*

- **show confidence** *by placing more toothpicks on the table*

Play continues until, following a match or a show of confidence, every player has responded, right round the circle.

Then all remaining players literally lay their cards on the table and the survivor with the lowest card wins.

Next, you can repeat the game, or play the variant Small Is Beautiful, and So Is Large, in which the winnings are split by the player with the lowest card and the player with the highest.

After the Mission is finished, you all take a moment to realise that it's the last one you'll ever complete together (though as Gregg points out, who knows how they might decide to mess with you on the final day).

- If you are Faithful, turn to **230**.

- If you are a Traitor, turn to **279**.

You leave the room and go to join the others, who are waiting to enter the Round Table, a dark, wood-panelled room with a large circular table in its centre. As you stride down the corridor, it feels absurd to even think it, but your Faithfulness seems to shine out of you. You see Elif and share what you hope is a genuine smile with her. She grips her notebook tightly. What will she write about you? 'I can sense a pure heart in this Contestant'? You smile to yourself. It seems absurd but you feel relaxed as you take a seat. Your conscience is clear. You are Faithful and anyone can see it just from looking at you.

- Turn to **257**.

When you get back inside, you head to the library, where Gabriel is playing Patience on his own. You stand and watch him for a moment. 'Any luck yet?' you ask. He sighs and puts the cards down. 'My head's not in the game.'

'Yes, I think we all feel a bit like that today,' you say. 'So what's the word on the street?'

'Well, we're slightly torn over Gregg as supremely sensitive or Traitor. And Tim seems *really* quite keen on Ruby or Precious as a potential Traitor now, because they both played their first Round Table brilliantly and there's now a thought that perhaps that's exactly what a smart Traitor would have done. Or not.'

'Very interesting,' you say. 'Especially as Ruby was just hypothesising that Tim and Anna would make sense as the last Traitors you'd ever suspect. One can't help but think of sharks and vending machines.'

Gabriel pulls a face but becomes calmer. 'God, that speech last night about vending machines. She was giddy, wasn't she? Actually, Tim or her isn't *impossible*, is it?' he says. 'Last time we voted out the last person any of us had suspected, she was a Traitor.' If Tim is going to get dragged into things, you don't want to be dragged down with him, but equally, you don't want to push him under the water. So you just shrug. 'OK,' says Gabriel. 'How about a game of Snap?' But luckily you're saved as word comes round that it's time for the day's Mission.

- Turn to **228**.

279

After the Mission, you all go and sit outside, looking out over the gardens, remembering those that have left the Castle.

The names that rush through your mind make it feel like a pinball machine. Not so long ago, you were trying to work out what Irwin was thinking, to analyse Amrit, to suss out Deb. You haven't even had a moment to give Tim another thought since the dust settled. And yet still it goes on. You think of Anna and her numbers, Jorge and his memory, David and his imaginary pub. You wonder what Nina is doing, and Teddy. You even slightly miss Laure (or maybe not).

- Turn to **67**.

280

'Well, I don't know about maths and models,' you say, 'but I certainly agree that we can't overlook irrational or selfish or stupid behaviour. Most of human history has been shaped by that, after all. I definitely think that this feels like one where the Traitors may have left themselves open. We just have to spot their mistake.'

You feel happy that you managed to make it clear that you were Faithful.

- Turn to **144**.

281

You write Gabriel. Ruby writes River. River has written Ruby. Gabriel has written Ruby's name.

'Ruby, you have been banished. Please tell us if you are Faithful or a Traitor.'

She steps forwards. 'I am so proud to have made it this far, even though I rejoined the game late. It's been a pleasure to get to know each and every one of you. But I'm afraid you made a mistake. I am a Faithful.' You groan along with everyone else as Ruby is quietly led away.

'So,' says your Host. 'The final three. Please step forwards and reveal whether you are Faithful or a Traitor.'

Gabriel steps forwards, smiling. 'When I came in here, I knew I just wanted to be me, whatever else happened. I wanted to be true to myself. And that's why I'm so happy to say that I am a Faithful.'

You step forwards solemnly. 'I'm so happy to have made it to the end. I've learnt so much here. That's why I'm delighted to say, I am a Faithful.' You and Gabriel beam at each other and you turn to River, who has a slightly odd look on her face.

River steps forwards and pauses. 'This game has been one of the most amazing experiences of my life. I've loved meeting everyone. Which is why I'm really sorry to say, I'm a Traitor.'

THE TRAITORS HAVE WON.

To play this day again, please turn to **113**. Better luck next time!

282

In the drawing room, a group are sitting on a sofa and armchairs. They don't seem to notice you.

'I just think some people are being very left brain about it, that's all,' says Rakayah.

You try and remember which side of the brain does what.

'Oh, that's just such classic male behaviour, though, isn't it?' says Laure and everyone nods, apart from Tim. 'Sorry, Tim,' says Laure.

'Oh, no need to apologise at all,' says Tim. 'At my age, you stop being a man, really, and you're more a kind of walking talking mushroom.' Tim is twinkly-eyed as he catches your gaze, but as previously, you catch an edge too.

Elif is scribbling away furiously in a notebook and notices you watching her.

'I'm getting all of this down,' she says. 'It's all going in "the computer", as I call it.'

You smile weakly as you get up to leave.

- Turn to **53**.

283

DAY 6

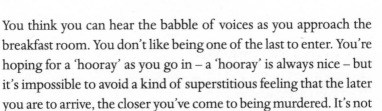

You think you can hear the babble of voices as you approach the breakfast room. You don't like being one of the last to enter. You're hoping for a 'hooray' as you go in – a 'hooray' is always nice – but it's impossible to avoid a kind of superstitious feeling that the later you are to arrive, the closer you've come to being murdered. It's not just you: River and Tim have told you they feel the same way too.

In any event, you get your cheer. The other thing about arriving later than most is that they've been able to keep in mind who hasn't yet come through the door; you, by contrast, cast your gaze around the room, trying to figure out who's not here yet.

Before you can work it out, voices are yelling, 'Laure's been murdered!' and 'It's Laure!'

Feeling sorry for Laure, you try to work out where to sit or stand. While you're doing this, you see a small group standing near the window. Gregg seems to be holding court and you think you can see heads turning to look at you and then away again.

In a moment of unease, you remember Gregg's observation yesterday that you had had enough of your conversation with Laure. You beetle over as quickly as possible. Rakayah nudges Gregg as you approach.

'Oh, hello. We were just saying,' Gregg greets you, 'that perhaps not everyone's as sorry as usual about this murder, God bless her!' Rakayah catches your eye and raises her eyebrows, you think in mild mockery of Gregg.

He's maintaining that jovial tone of his, but the others look at you again at this point. Up to now you had dismissed Gregg as a slightly simple creature, mainly taken up with mooning after Deb. You'll clearly need to keep more of an eye on him. In the meantime, how to react?

What do you do?

- Laugh it off. Turn to **117**.

- Explain that you had no problem with Laure. Turn to **79**.

Outside, it has stopped raining and it smells of wet earth and lavender. You perch on the steps like you did that first day, even though they're slightly damp.

'Poor Gregg,' says River, as you all watch him trudge away through the grounds with the weight of the world on his shoulders.

'Yeah, it's weird, isn't it?' says Ruby. 'Even though Nina was a Traitor, he's taken it hard. Traitor guilt perhaps?'

'Yes, maybe he's feeling guilty about knocking off one of his own,' says Precious.

'That's interesting. On the other hand, I think we were all so shocked that Nina was a Traitor,' says River, taking her shoes off and stretching her toes out. She looks up at you.

'It's such a shock,' you say. 'I can only speak for myself but I certainly didn't have Nina on my list until the lie was revealed. Even now, I can't imagine anyone who's left being a Traitor.'

'Totally,' says River, dreamily. 'Do you remember when we used to fill up all of these steps pretty much? Now there's only a few of us rattling around in the Castle.' You all stare into the distance.

'Ok, I'm going to say it just because I have to,' says Ruby. 'Gregg is behaving weirdly. But then he's a weird guy. Wouldn't Anna and Tim actually be the perfect Traitors? Tim is basically the uncle we all wish we had, and has Anna ever even had her name written once? And that was a weird speech last night. Wasn't she a bit too happy about Nina going? That smacks of relief to me.'

Both you and River automatically laugh. 'Lovely Tim?!' says River. But she looks around at everyone as they take a moment. She can see they're taking it seriously and you see her starting to think too.

- Turn to **34**.

285

You look down at the table and when River realises that you're not going to help her, her mouth sets in a straight line. She says that she's been getting funny vibes off you all day, like you've been keeping a secret for the last couple of days. Oh dear. She points out several times throughout the day when you have behaved oddly, with an eye honed by expertise. You suddenly understand the phrase 'set a thief to catch a thief' in a whole new light.

Gabriel and Tim both agree you have been different. Ruby is watching you intently. Gregg is looking at you calmly, as he agrees too. Judas.

You need to bring this back around or it is going to be all they talk about tonight. You try to give a passionate defence of yourself, but even you can hear it sounds weak.

River seizes upon that and – even you have to admit – makes a pretty good case for why at this stage in the game everyone has to trust their guts on this stuff.

When it's time for people to hold up names, you vote for River and are gratified to see that Gabriel does too. Too late, you realise that River and Tim clearly saw you as a pawn to sacrifice at a later date. Well played by them.

'Well, let's see if you've made the right decision,' says your Host. 'Are you Faithful or a Traitor?'

You can't believe how quickly you wilted under the pressure of being a Traitor.

You take a moment. 'I'm a Traitor,' you say. You leave to the sound of the room cheering, desperately wanting them to know that you weren't always a Traitor, but knowing they never will.

YOU HAVE BEEN BANISHED.

To play this day again, please turn to **18**. Better luck next time!

286

There's a little gang here. River is in full flow. 'Think about it. We're all on the lookout for liars. And then David basically confesses to being one. It's totally understandable that we thought he was a Traitor.'

You agree: 'And likewise, Alexis drew a target on her back as soon as she showed the Traitors that people were willing to be swayed by her.'

'Right,' agrees River. 'I reckon they still feel at this stage that there are enough people that it's about taking out the obvious threats.'

'I think you're right,' observes Deb. 'So what we need to do is watch out for physical tells like—'

'—like being really cold-hearted and ruthless!' River completes Deb's sentence. 'So, Deb, what are those tells?'

It seems to you that this may not have been what Deb had in mind, but she's always happy to talk body language.

'Right, you know how a smile isn't just this,' she says, doing a funny little smirk, 'it should go all the way to the eyes?' She gives an over-the-top example. Others join in. 'Well, a cold-hearted person, their smile stops halfway. Like this.' She does a sort of half-smile and it's true – for a moment she resembles one of those movie characters that turns out to be a serial killer.

The conversation turns to more general chitchat and you walk off across the grounds, waving to Deb.

- Turn to **227**.

287

Inside, it feels suddenly very dark compared to the bright sun out-side. You wander about for a while without seeing anyone, until you reach a room and see Gabriel asleep on one of the sofas. You turn to tiptoe back out again but the floorboard squeaks.

'I'm just resting my eyes!' he calls.

'I absolutely don't want to disturb you,' you say.

'Just don't expect me to have any useful theories. I didn't sleep at all last night and I'm utterly clueless.'

You tell him that pretty much everyone feels like that.

'Actually,' he says, 'I know I'm definitely Faithful. And I'm almost entirely sure you are. Other than that, flip a coin. Someone we trust is lying.'

You are glad that Gabriel has his eyes closed, or you feel sure he'd notice your face burning red with a surprising amount of shame. Even though you remind yourself that you haven't been lying the entire time, it feels like you're lying to people you now consider friends.

You chat for a bit about how everyone responded to the revelation that Tim was a Traitor. You are aware of wanting to not be overly protective of River and you suggest that Gregg would have taken his mentor figure lying to him hard. You make a mental note to try and flag this to River.

'Well, I'll leave you to it,' you say, and Gabriel salutes goodbye.

Then word comes around that it's time for the final Mission.

- Turn to **276**.

BONUS GAME

THE KING'S NEW GAME

You need: pens and a large number of index cards (or pieces of paper cut to index-card size), a creative spirit

Players: three or more

> You are asked to imagine that the King has decreed that a new game must be created for his birthday.
>
> His Majesty has said only that it must be a brand-new game and that it should involve cards (but, he has insisted, not playing cards).
>
> It is now your task to create this game.
>
> All players should take ten minutes to create three cards. They should give each card a name, write down what the effect of playing that card is, and give at least a cursory illustration. The game works best if players are given no further instruction, but if anyone is really stuck, here are a few tips.*
>
> * A card might say something like 'Take two cards from any other players' or 'Gain 100 coins' or 'Go to prison for three turns'.

The cards are then shuffled and dealt. The player to the dealer's left chooses a card to play. Depending on what is written on the card, they might be playing it 'to themselves', 'to another player', 'to the group', and so on. The card will almost certainly raise a question about how the game works, which should be answered by the person playing it. If the card is one that players need to remember, it stays face up on the table. Otherwise, it goes to a discard pile.

At any point, any player may take another blank index card and create a new game card. They might play it, award it to another player or put it in a face-down pile for a future deal. This is to be determined by the players.

Ideally, players will adapt the developing rules and create new cards which combine with the existing ones to make a satisfying game.

The game is over according to whatever rule for ending the game the players decide.

Have fun!

As the game finishes, you are sent for in the Round Table.

- If you are Faithful, turn to **242**.

- If you are a Traitor, turn to **160**.

When it is your turn to speak, you address Gabriel. 'Gabriel, I know you thought I was aggressive back there, and I know someone like you doesn't respond well to that. But I swear to you that it comes from passion. I am a Faithful.'

River says pretty much the same thing, but is it just you, or does the pleading not quite reach her eyes?

'Now it is time for you to vote again,' says your Host.

This time, you write River. Ruby writes River. River has written your name. Gabriel has changed his mind and written River's name.

'River, you have been banished. Please tell us if you are Faithful or a Traitor.'

She steps forwards. 'This game has been one of the most amazing experiences of my life. I've loved meeting everyone. Which is why I'm really happy for you because I am a Traitor.' There are gasps and nervous smiles as River is quietly led away.

'So,' says your Host. 'The final three. Please step forwards and reveal whether you are Faithful or a Traitor.'

Gabriel steps forwards, smiling. 'When I came in here, I knew I just wanted to be me, whatever else happened. I wanted to be true to myself. And that's why I'm so happy to say that I am a Faithful.'

Ruby steps forwards solemnly. 'I am so proud to have made it this far, even though I rejoined the game late. It's been a pleasure to get to know each and every one of you. That's why I'm so happy to say, I am a Faithful.'

You step forwards and pause. 'I'm so happy to have made it to the end. I've learnt so much here. That's why I'm delighted to say, I am a Faithful.'

'Congratulations, Faithfuls, you have won!'

YOU HAVE WON.

290

Finally it's your turn and you are called inside. You are sitting before your Host as they fire questions at you. 'I need to know if you have what it takes to be a Traitor.'

You are genuinely conflicted. No one likes to think of themselves as untrustworthy. But at least as a Traitor you wouldn't be murdered. Wouldn't you rather be banished than murdered?

Would you have what it takes to lie to everyone around you, to always be looking over your shoulder, to betray their trust? Already, everyone you have spoken to has said they could never be a Traitor. But they would say that, wouldn't they. And every decision has consequences. Is it possible to give the wrong answer?

What do you do?

- Tell your Host you could be a Traitor. Turn to **194**.

- Tell your Host you could only ever be Faithful. Turn to **277**.

291

Deb looks more upset than the others. 'It doesn't add up,' she reckons. 'Amrit's not like someone who's been leading the charges at Round Tables.' Everyone is pottering about, making drinks. Tim tells someone how strong he wants his tea. At this point you'd be disappointed if he didn't.

'Sure,' agrees Isla. 'He wasn't a finger pointer. He just wasn't.'

Gabriel says he's pretty sure there must be a reason. 'And the most obvious thing, the most obvious reason to murder someone, is if they're on to you. Even if you haven't said so on a big stage, you know, like Round Table.'

So, you're all wondering: who did Amrit suspect? And Isla's the one who would know.

'That's the funny thing,' she says. 'The only person he talked about being a Traitor . . . was me. I mean, he said it like he was kidding, but I think he felt he knew me well enough that he'd be able to tell from my reaction. He honestly didn't mention anyone else. Not when I was talking with him, anyway.' You are surprised that Isla would draw attention to herself in this way and you catch Gabriel and Tim pulling a face too. If she is a Traitor, she's an incredibly bold one.

River thinks that the Traitors are 'super devious'. To commit a murder like this, 'when we can't draw anything from it', is . . . she looks for the word, '. . . like I say, devious'.

Tim's take is that it was 'a clever murder'. 'Because they know it's shocking. Confusing. Hurtful. You pick someone who we'll tie ourselves in knots trying to work out why them. It's the cat and we're the pigeons. And if there's one thing I do know, it's pigeons.'

You spend a quiet morning chatting until your Host arrives and tells you it's time for the day's Mission.

- Turn to **108**.

292

'I'll go first this time,' you say. 'And it was actually something you said earlier, Ruby, that made me think of this.' She has a look of apprehension on her face. 'You said that it was hard to know what normal behaviour was in this environment. And that got me thinking that you've had an advantage coming in late, as we haven't got to know you yet. You've led the charge a couple of times against people who've turned out to be Traitors. But who knows if you just want to win on your own? I look at you and I see a very intelligent, capable person, who is playing this game brilliantly. A perfect Traitor. I could be wrong, but I have to say it.'

Ruby is shocked for a moment, before she goes on the offensive. She points out how illogical it would be for her to enter the Castle as a Traitor and then proceed to wipe out her fellow Traitors. She points out that everyone has got to know her a bit by now and knows she's logical and pragmatic.

She seems genuinely disappointed that you've turned on her like this and concludes that the only reason for it must be that you are desperately trying to distract people from your own increasingly erratic behaviour. She says that this behaviour has made up her mind. You are a Traitor.

Gabriel says he's surprised by your accusation as this wasn't what you were saying earlier. River agrees that this feels like it bears little relationship to conversations you had earlier. Gregg can clearly see which way the wind is blowing and says something vague about seeing everyone's point of view.

When the names are written, you vote for Ruby, but everyone else votes for you. To come so close but so far from winning burns. You can't help but feel like you really messed up when it mattered the most.

'I am . . . a Faithful,' you say.

YOU HAVE BEEN BANISHED.

To play this day again, please turn to **113**. Better luck next time!

293

As you get to the drawing room, several people are just leaving, with only Elif left, who is scribbling into a notebook. She looks up when you enter. 'Oh hello,' she says. 'It's you. Come and sit down.'

You sit quietly, while she finishes what she's writing. 'Sorry about that,' she says. 'If I don't write it down, I'll forget. I call it "the computer".' She looks at you and you realise she expects a response.

'Well, I hope it doesn't break,' you say. 'So I hear there's a bit of a schism in the group already, between the forces of reason and feeling.'

'Oh, tell me about it,' says Elif. 'Rakayah was literally just saying that to Laure and River and me, and lovely Tim.' You make a wincing face. 'But Tim said that was fine because at his age, he's basically a mushroom.'

'Was it some sort of fun guy joke?' you ask.

'Don't think so,' says Elif, checking back in her book, frowning.

Just then, Gabriel puts his head around the door and says it's time for the Mission.

- Turn to **48**.

294

As you descend the stairs, Teddy's coming up but he does a 180-degree turn when he sees you, and waits for you at the bottom.

'Know what we found out this morning?' he says quietly. 'Gregg's a crime novelist.'

'Ooh, how's that gone down?' you ask.

'Well, River is very suspicious! I mean, it is allowed, and I don't see anything wrong with it myself. He said he doesn't write the sorts of books that would be useful, but what I do find weird is him not saying. You know, I tell people anything they want to know about me, and some things they don't, that's just me. There's something not right about how vague he was when we met. You know? I feel like us Faithfuls have all been really upfront with each other.'

You're not one hundred per cent sure you agree but you nod your head gamely. Teddy seems to be the sort of person who likes it when people agree with him. But if yesterday taught you anything, it's that someone else can lead a charge against Gregg.

As you walk back along the corridor, someone shouts out to ask if anyone is up for a game of cards in the library and you wander over.

- Turn to **156**.

295

DAY 8

'Is it too much to hope that no one will be murdered again this morning? It is, isn't it?' says River sombrely, poking at her plate. You know things are bad when even she is down in the dumps. Gabriel gives her hand a squeeze.

'I don't think we'll be that lucky,' you say. There's the familiar knock on the door, as Nina, Teddy, Tim and Gregg enter. The room suddenly seems sparsely populated. It is a cloudy day and no one seems very inclined to chat. Even Tim saying he wants his tea strong enough to stand a spoon up in it only gets a half-hearted cheer.

It's between Anna and Jorge. And then there's a knock as Anna comes in. As ever, there's a balancing act, as people try to reassure the person who has survived while being appropriately sad about the person who hasn't.

'Oh Jorge,' says Gabriel.

'Oh man, oh man,' is Teddy's response.

The conversation turns to why, and everyone is of one mind that Jorge's undoing was his impressive memory, and perhaps the sense that he was bearing up better than everyone else. For once, Anna doesn't have any risk-related facts to share.

'Smart move to keep morale low,' says Tim, shaking his head.

'Doesn't feel right,' reckons Nina. 'I thought Jorge would always be here.'

'Yeah,' agrees Teddy. 'No one is safe from them.'

Nina isn't her usual self and seems reserved.

What do you do?

- Tell Nina you feel bad about last night. Turn to **302**.

- Leave it and hope it gets forgotten. Turn to **8**.

296

You're by no means alone as you raise your hand to move to the vote.

'I suppose we have to choose someone,' chuckles Tim. Again, you think he's probably feeling that if he makes it through this Round Table, he may not get nominated again for a little while.

Your Host announces, 'We will abide by your decision. And also, of course, by the more important decision you are about to make. It is time to carry out your first banishment. Please write down who you think should leave the game.'

Suddenly it all seems very real. In a few moments' time, someone will leave the room, and the game, for good. You ask yourself who's acting most like a Traitor, and while of course all three players might be innocent, Steve-O is the one who seems most defensive.

As those ahead of you read out the name they've written down, almost everyone has written Steve-O. When it's your time to justify it, you just say, 'I had to write someone, I'm sorry.' Most people seem to have felt the same. River and Laure actually vote for Tim, but other than that, it's time for Steve-O to leave. It's a big moment, watching him stand. His upper lip is trembling.

'Steve-O,' intones your Host. 'You have been banished. Before you leave the Castle, it's time to reveal whether you're Faithful or a Traitor.'

'I'd just like to say,' offers Steve-O, 'I honestly thought I'd be here longer than this. I wasn't sure I'd win, but this . . .' He peters out. 'You messed up, guys. I'm a Faithful. Or was.'

'Oh no!' barks Rakayah.

'This is on me, guys, I'm sorry, I rushed things,' offers Irwin. 'Steve-O, you're right, I'm so sorry, mate.'

- Turn to **244**.

297

You try to convince the room that Gregg's behaviour is the truly suspect thing here, and explain that you didn't even know the actual secret, just that there *was* a secret. But Gregg is extremely persuasive as the simple man caught in a moral dilemma, and somehow it's you and Nina who are the units of deceit.

Then Tim and River sadly and regretfully say that it's one too many times that you're at the centre of the drama. And Anna weighs in and says that, mathematically, the only solution they haven't tried is you. Even Nina has clearly sensed which way the wind is blowing because she says that she's angry at Gregg for betraying her confidence, but that he is telling the truth about what she told him. Whereas she can't help but feel that keeping secrets like you have is the sign of someone with something to hide.

As the names are revealed, it's a three-way split between you, Gregg and Nina. But as River and Tim both hold up your name one after the other, it's you by one vote.

As your Host welcomes you to tell them whether you're a Traitor or Faithful, you can't hide the bitterness in your voice as you tell them they have banished another Faithful.

YOU HAVE BEEN BANISHED.

To play this day again, please turn to **258**. Better luck next time!

298

The library is empty apart from the four of you, as you settle onto sofas.

'We didn't mean to be so dramatic,' says Jorge, flashing his bright teeth.

'No, not at all,' says Deb. 'It's just that earlier I was talking to Alexis and she said something I thought was really interesting, and then she said that it came out of a conversation with you, so I wanted to check.' Gregg doesn't say anything, just gazes happily at Deb. You're starting to understand what everyone means.

'Was it you?'

'Depends what *it* is,' you say.

'Well, Alexis was saying that we need to stop thinking the Traitors are going to be obvious, and think about double bluffs and even triple bluffs.'

'And I totally agree,' says Jorge.

What do you do?

- Take credit for the theory. Turn to **90**.
- Play down your role and say it was Alexis's idea really. Turn to **150**.

299

Well done, you're right. Like everyone else, you are (for the purposes of this activity) either a truth-teller or a liar. If you're a liar, then since Gabriel is pointing at you, a truth-teller is pointing at a liar. The only other possibility is that you are a truth-teller, and since you're pointing at River, then a truth-teller is pointing at a liar. Return to **228**.

300

Inside, it feels suddenly very dark compared to the bright sun outside. You wander about for a while without seeing anyone, until you reach a room and see Gabriel asleep on one of the sofas. You turn to tiptoe back out again but the floorboard squeaks.

'I'm just resting my eyes!' he calls.

'I absolutely don't want to disturb you,' you say.

'Just don't expect me to have any useful theories. I didn't sleep at all last night and I'm utterly clueless.'

You tell him that pretty much everyone feels like that.

'Actually,' he says, 'I know I'm definitely a Faithful. And I'm almost entirely sure you are. Other than that, flip a coin. Someone we trust is lying.'

It feels nice that at least one person has your back and you agree that you're sure Gabriel is Faithful too, with just the tiniest voice in the back of your head saying that's exactly what a Traitor would be doing – forming multiple alliances and flattering people into reciprocating.

You chat for a bit about Gregg still seeming quiet since the revelation that Tim was a Traitor. You both think it's likely that he saw Tim as a mentor figure.

Then word comes around that it's time for the Mission.

- Turn to **276**.

301

There's still a couple of people on the steps when you get back. You smile to Deb as you approach.

'You see, now that's a proper smile! Goes right to the eyes.' Deb explains she was just telling everyone how a Traitor won't be able to smile properly, that it will stop at their eyes. You nod along, wondering where she gets this stuff from and enjoying the sunshine.

All too soon though it's time to head inside, where your Host is waiting for you.

'It's Mission time again.' You have to admit, you've actually grown quite fond of these moments when everyone has the same aims. For once, you can just let your guard down and only worry about whether or not you're going to muck up the Mission.

- Turn to **96**.

302

You go and sit next to Nina.

As soon as you apologise for your role, she waves her hand. 'All part of the game. Deb certainly wouldn't hold any grudges.'

You are slightly surprised by this lack of emotion, but you put it down to shock.

'It actually makes me feel like I'm less likely to be banished. At least for a couple of nights anyway. Either that or more likely.' Something about her expression causes you to laugh, and then both of you are laughing at the absurdity of it.

'Yes,' you gasp. 'One of the two. Or maybe it'll make no difference at all.'

- Turn to **180**.

You hear the babble of voices coming from the library, so you head over.

'Too hot out there!' you say as you enter. 'This is much more sensible. What have I missed?'

'Oh, it's been very high octane in here,' says Tim. 'We've been having a little Castle book club chat.'

Ruby has a leather-bound book open on her lap. 'To be honest, I'm just glad when something I'm reading isn't some sort of peer-reviewed study.'

'And I was just saying that it was only recently that I really started reading,' says Tim, settling into an armchair. 'I didn't enjoy school but now I always have about three books on the go.'

'I'm just going to put this out there with no comment,' says Ruby, 'but I am finding myself more and more interested by how Gregg is behaving.' There is a lot of nodding and Tim taps his nose. Everyone agrees to keep an eye on Gregg.

River is just watching and listening to you all with a half-smile on her face. You think again how odd it is that the odds are that one of them is a Traitor. All your time in the Castle so far has made you realise how hard it is to tell if someone is lying.

All of you settle back into a conversation about your favourite books before the call goes round there's a game breaking out in the next room. You bid your farewells and head in.

- Turn to **216**.

304

There is no great desire to laugh and make merry tonight. Everyone goes through the motions but Nina makes her excuses early and heads up to bed.

Jorge does his best to try and make everyone feel better about what happened. But it's a relief when the gong sounds and you can go up to your room.

For the first time, you wonder if perhaps it might be a mercy to leave. The emotional highs and lows are simply too much. You close your eyes wearily, not even listening for footsteps in the corridor.

- Turn to **295**.

305

You look Rakayah in the eye and tell her that this isn't true. You relate the conversation you had with Gregg and say that you're disappointed that he's been sharing it without you there.

'Although you are talking behind his back,' notes Tim. 'But fair's fair, though, you need to defend yourself.'

'So you're basically saying Gregg's a Traitor,' infers Teddy.

You aren't, but you don't want to sound too defensive. Plus it's never easy to interject when Teddy's warming to a theme.

'Could be,' says Tim. 'Let's see. Pros and cons. Pros: you get people talking about each other, starting to suspect each other. But. Major con. Someone's gonna notice, 'specially as the group gets smaller.

And then what you've done is draw attention to yourself. Nope. Not buying it, I'm afraid.'

'I agree, Tim,' says Rakayah.

So now you do think you need to say that you're not accusing Gregg of anything other than getting the wrong end of the stick. It all sounds a bit weaker than you'd like.

It's almost time for Round Table.

What do you do?

- Enter with confidence, greeting people loudly. Turn to **4**.

- Keep a lower profile. Turn to **147**.

306

You write River. Ruby writes River. River has written Ruby's name. Gabriel has written your name.

'River, you have been banished. Please tell us if you are Faithful or a Traitor.'

She steps forwards. 'This game has been one of the most amazing experiences of my life. I've loved meeting everyone. Which is why I'm really happy for you because I am a Traitor.' Ruby can't help but yelp with joy as River is quietly led away. You feel yourself smiling. Surely there can't be a final twist. Can there?!

'So,' says your Host. 'The final three. Please step forwards and reveal whether you are Faithful or a Traitor.'

Gabriel steps forwards, smiling. 'When I came in here, I knew I just wanted to be me, whatever else happened. I wanted to be true to myself. And that's why I'm so happy to say that I am a Faithful.'

You step forwards solemnly. 'I'm so happy to have made it to the end. I've learnt so much here. That's why I'm delighted to say, I am a Faithful.'

Ruby steps forwards and pauses. 'I am so proud to have made it this far, even though I rejoined the game late. It's been a pleasure to get to know each and every one of you. That's why I'm so happy to say, I am a Faithful.'

Everyone hugs and cheers as you all realise what this means.

YOU HAVE WON.

307

You stay sitting at the Round Table, solemn and downbeat. Ruby touches your arm. 'It made sense to me too,' she says.

Your Host steps forwards. 'So you banished a Faithful. Why? Did you make the wrong decision or are there just no more Traitors left? The game is now in your hands. You now face a choice. You can unanimously decide to end the game now. If you believe there is a Traitor in your midst, you must banish again. You will need to join me out front for your final task. And a reminder. If there is even one Traitor among you, they have won.'

You realise there is one final chance to speak to the room and River clearly feels the same. 'Well, I suppose one of us needs to say something. Personally, I'm certain on one person – me. And I'm ninety-five per cent sure on Gabriel. You two, I am really not sure about if I'm honest.' There is that brief flicker of annoyance on Ruby's face as River speaks, which you wonder if she's aware of.

There is a last opportunity to say something.

What do you do?

- Leap in. Turn to **11**.

- Hang back. Turn to **20**.

308

After a shocked group talk about David and his fictional pub, and the fact you've sent another Faithful home, several people apologise for their false accusations. You are happy to escape the spotlight for now. There are clearly a lot of theories flying about, but you just want to go to bed. That was too close for comfort.

You sleep fitfully, your dreams full of danger. But you wake to a bright morning.

- Turn to **31**.

You test it out in your mind and it suddenly clicks.

'I'm not sure what this means, but has anyone noticed that Teddy has gone from constantly putting himself in the Traitors' shoes, to actively avoiding it at every opportunity, and he's suddenly obsessed with telling us he's Faithful. I don't know if it's a strategy or if he's lost his bottle, but it's clear as day.'

As soon as you've said it, you realise other people have noticed it. They look at you with a dawning realisation.

Then Teddy looks at you sharply. 'I don't know about anyone else but it's not so much a change, more that you're always in the frame but somehow never get banished. And pretty much every time, we banish the wrong people. Maybe we need to stop making that mistake.'

But it doesn't catch. It just reads like revenge, and the sharpness of the attack looks like a mask slipping even more. Gregg jumps in to remind everyone that it was you who had basically got rid of Rakayah, the only success you've had.

It's like dominoes falling as it is time for people to vote. You notice with a sense of satisfaction that even Precious and Ruby have been swayed by your argument.

'Well, Teddy, time to bare your soul and tell us. Are you Faithful or a Traitor?'

He stands, with one eyebrow raised. 'I am . . . a Traitor.'

There is an audible whoop as Teddy leaves the room.

YOU HAVE BANISHED A TRAITOR.

- Turn to **208**.

310

You leave the drawing room and head out towards the welcoming bright sunlight of the back door. As you reach the steps, you see Ruby heading towards you, and River walking off towards the lake. They've obviously been enjoying a stroll in the sunlight. If it had been you alone with Ruby, you would have wilted. Perhaps that's why River is off on her own?

'Hallooo,' you call. Ruby is slightly out of breath as she reaches you.

'River and I just found the most incredible walled garden back there,' she says. 'There's strawberries and lettuces, loads of delicious looking stuff.' You both sit down on the steps.

'Well, Gabriel and I are stumped,' you say after a few seconds.

'River and I were literally just saying that,' says Ruby. 'I thought I'd be smart and watch really closely how people acted at the last couple of banishments but I didn't spot anything. You try and think back, to see if there's anything that stands out. But who knows what normal behaviour is in such an abnormal situation.'

You chat for a bit about how weird it is that at least one of you is a Traitor, and how this has changed what you think about how people lie. You had both previously thought you were good judges of whether someone was lying or not, but you've realised that you're not at all. The whole time you're sure she can tell how much you're second-guessing every answer.

As you're sitting there, Gregg joins you. 'Phew, it's like the *Mary Celeste* in there. For a while I thought I was the only one left and that was all part of it. I started getting a bit panicky.'

After a few more minutes you decide to head back inside and see if you can find the others. It's almost time for the last Mission.

- Turn to **276**.

311

Everyone returns from the Mission energised and excited, but it's sobering to suddenly remember you're not actually all one team. You find yourself in a small group including River (South London, 32) and Deb, as they hold forth on how strange it is that there are now Traitors among you. Luke is talking loudly about how he could never be a Traitor. 'In fact,' he says, 'the only thing I know for sure is that I'm a Faithful.' Whereas Nina is expressing sympathy for them. 'After all, it's going to be so hard lying to people.' Teddy says that everyone has to start thinking like a Traitor to catch them.

Rakayah keeps repeating, 'I just can't get over the fact that someone is going to get murdered tonight.'

You're sitting in contented silence, nodding along, when suddenly Tim turns to you. 'What do you think?'

What do you do?

- Speak up and give your theories about the game. After all, you need to prove your value for the alliances to come. Turn to **254**.

- Offer a platitude. There's no point planting your flag in the sand until you know the lie of the land a little more. Turn to **163**.

312

You try to look back out at the room steadily, but River quietly mentions that you also knew the secret. And that's all the invitation Deb needs to start speaking first.

'I'm sorry, I know we told a lie and that's bad.' She looks at you. 'But this is about the fourth time now you've been at the centre of things, whispering in people's ears. We've all realised that Traitors are manipulating us, guiding us? Well, that's one hundred per cent you. I can hand on my heart say that this lie didn't benefit me and that I'm a Faithful, but I just don't think you can say the same.'

Even Nina manages to rally. 'I thought we were good enough friends that you would come and talk to me about this, but the fact that you didn't and told tales behind my back is really hurtful.'

And that seems to be the final nail in the coffin. The room's sense of hurt about being told a lie for so long seems to be transformed into anger at you. Suddenly everyone is remembering times that you've been there skulking in the shadows.

You don't really need to look at the names as they come up to know that yours will be written the most. As you stand to tell them they have made a mistake, you wonder if they will even care. There was something primal at work there. They needed a scapegoat and it was you.

YOU HAVE BEEN BANISHED.

To play this day again, please turn to **24**. Better luck next time!